Book-k

STAGE II

CONTINUING THE COURSE BEGUN IN
BOOK-KEEPING, STAGE I, TO THE
INTERMEDIATE STAGE

A. J. Favell, B.Sc. (Econ.)

THIRD EDITION

F. C. Thurling, B.A. (Hons.), A.C.I.S.

Principal, Tottenham Technical College

PITMAN

PITMAN BOOKS LIMITED
128 Long Acre, London WC2E 9AN

Associated Companies
Pitman Publishing Pty Ltd, Melbourne
Pitman Publishing New Zealand Ltd, Wellington

© Lilian Favell 1959, 1969

Third edition 1969
Reprinted 1971, 1972, 1973 (twice), 1976, 1978, 1980, 1982

Text set in 10/11 pt Monotype Times New Roman, printed and bound
in Great Britain at The Pitman Press, Bath

ISBN 0 273 40281 1

PUBLISHERS' PREFACE TO THIRD EDITION

DEMAND for this book has been gratifyingly consistent over the years. Conversion to decimal currency has given us the opportunity to make improvements to the text, and it is hoped that the book will continue to be held in high regard.

PREFACE TO SECOND EDITION

THE revision of this book was made necessary chiefly because of changes in certain public examination syllabuses and the consequent necessity to transfer much *Stage II* matter to *Stage I*. This new edition follows naturally upon the revision of *Book-keeping, Stage I*.

The opportunity has been taken to bring some textual matter and many exercises up to date, and the Key to the exercises in this volume has also been revised.

F. C. T.

PREFACE TO FIRST EDITION

THIS volume continues the exposition in *Book-keeping, Stage I*, to the intermediate stage of the subject, and should meet the needs of the many teachers who have found that *Book-keeping, Stage I*, provides a sound teaching method, and who desire to carry their students further in the subject on similar lines.

It is desired to acknowledge the kind permission to use past examination papers granted by the various Examining Bodies, and my thanks are due to Mr. C. H. Mears, F.S.A.A., for his kindness in reading the manuscript.

A. J. F.

ABBREVIATIONS

N.C.T.E.C. = Northern Counties Technical Examinations Council.
R.S.A.   = Royal Society of Arts.
U.E.I.   = Union of Educational Institutions.
U.L.C.I.   = Union of Lancashire and Cheshire Institutes.

CONTENTS

CHAPTER I

MANUFACTURING ACCOUNTS

STUDENTS can be expected to have a fairly clear conception at this stage in their studies of the significance of the separate Trading Account and Profit and Loss Account.

They will realize that the intention in drawing up a Trading Account is to find the profit made on the buying and selling of goods, taking into account any matters which *directly* affect the turnover or total sales. The intention in drawing up a Profit and Loss Account is to find the real or actual profit by adding to the trading (or gross) profit, obtained from the Trading Account, any non-trading profit (e.g. Discount Received) and by deducting all *indirect* expenses (e.g. Discount Allowed) which will include expenses of administration.

It is possible, of course, to put all the above into *one* account instead of two, but we should then have the net profit only. The two accounts facilitate the comparison of results from year to year and make more obvious where any weakness lies. The gross profit, for example, should bear more or less the same relation to total sales, or turnover, from year to year. Any violent changes in the relationship should indicate that some factor requires investigating. It may indicate that the valuation of the stock is at fault or that, with a correct valuation, the stock is not complete, or that some loss has occurred through theft or other means. Fluctuation in the rate of gross profit to sales can also indicate faulty buying and that the purchases during the period have been made at a higher figure. If this was unavoidable then it may become necessary to introduce a new sales policy to meet the altered conditions.

The separate Profit and Loss Account enables a year-to-year comparison to be made of the indirect expenses to the net profit, gross profit, and turnover. An increase in the ratio of these expenses to turnover more than proportional to any increase in sales would clearly demand investigation.

To ensure valid comparison it is essential that the Trading and Profit and Loss Accounts should be compiled on a basis consistent from year to year. If there is doubt whether certain items are to be regarded as a direct or an indirect expense (e.g. Depreciation) a decision must be made and adhered to thereafter.

The Manufacturing Account

A manufacturing concern produces finished goods from raw materials and sells them, whereas a trading concern buys its goods ready made and sells them.

The former performs the extra functions of producing or manufacturing goods and will be concerned to show the cost of production in a Working or Production or Manufacturing Account. This cost of production will be transferred (as the equivalent of "Purchases" in the non-manufacturing organization) to the Trading Account wherein will be found, as was said earlier, all the *direct* trading expenses, that is, the cost of warehousing the finished goods and the cost of their distribution, etc.

Confusion may arise because some smaller manufacturers do not keep separate Manufacturing Accounts but include all production expenses in the Trading Account. If this is done, then strictly speaking such an account is neither a Trading nor a Manufacturing Account though both terms, erroneously regarded as synonymous, may be used in describing it.

The Manufacturing Account, in showing the cost of production, will show the opening and closing stocks of raw materials, the purchases of raw materials, wages of the factory workers and other production expenses such as fuel, lighting, power, and factory rent. Depreciation of factory machinery, tools, and equipment is frequently put here rather than in the Profit and Loss Account.

An additional item will be unfinished or partly finished goods. These are valued at the beginning and at the end of each trading or accounting period—the value will be made up of the cost of materials plus the cost of labour consumed thus far—and entered in a separate account in the same way as the stock of finished goods, with which the student is already familiar. Thus the closing stock of unfinished goods should be credited to Manufacturing Account (or deducted from the debit side—see example p. 4) and debited to Stock of Unfinished Goods Account: the opening stock of unfinished goods should be debited to Manufacturing Account and credited to Stock of Unfinished Goods Account. The balance of the account will appear on the Balance Sheet with the other stocks—those of raw materials and finished goods.

The nature of unfinished goods will naturally vary according to the product and will be found in most Trial Balances and Balance Sheets as Work in Progress rather than as Unfinished Goods. Engineering and building firms working to contracts will frequently classify unfinished goods as Uncompleted Contracts. Whatever name is given, all partly-finished work will be dealt with in the way described.

Below is an example and a variation of a Manufacturing Account followed by the Trading Account.

MANUFACTURING ACCOUNT

FOR THE YEAR ENDED 31ST DECEMBER, 19..

	£		£
To Stock of Raw Materials (at start)	3,000	By Stock of Raw Materials (at close)	4,000
,, Work in Progress (partly-manufactured goods at start)	5,000	,, Work in Progress (at close)	5,500
,, Purchases of Raw Materials (*less* returns)	25,000	,, Balance—being cost of production of finished goods —transferred to Trading Account	64,800
,, Carriage Inwards (on Raw Materials)	800		
,, Production Wages	30,000		
,, Factory Power and Light	2,500		
,, Factory Expenses	8,000		
	£74,300		£74,300

By deducting the closing stock of Raw Materials from the debit side, the cost of production can still be found with the useful additional information of the *cost of goods consumed*. (See below.)

MANUFACTURING ACCOUNT

FOR THE YEAR ENDED 31ST DECEMBER, 19..

	£	£		£
To Stock of Raw			By Work in Progress, 31st Dec .	5,500
,, Materials, 1st Jan . . .	3,000		,, Cost of Production of Finished Goods trans-ferred to Trading Account	64,800
,, Purchases of Raw Materials (*less* returns) . .	25,000			
	28,000			
Less Stock of Raw Materials, 31st Dec . . .	4,000			
,, Raw Materials consumed . .		24,000		
,, Work in Progress, 1st Jan . . .		5,000		
,, Carriage Inwards .		800		
,, Production Wages .		30,000		
,, Factory Power and Light . . .		2,500		
,, Factory Expenses .		8,000		
		£70,300		£70,300

TRADING ACCOUNT

FOR THE YEAR ENDED 31ST DECEMBER, 19..

	£		£
To Stock of Finished Goods . (at start)	12,000	By Sales (*less* returns) . .	100,000
,, Cost of Production transferred from Manufacturing Account . . .	64,800	,, Stock of Finished Goods (at close) . .	15,000
,, Purchases of Finished Goods (*less* returns) . . .	2,500		
,, Trading Expenses . . .	5,000		
,, Gross Profit to Profit and Loss Account . . .	30,700		
	£115,000		£115,000

On the debit side of the Balance Sheet, under *Current Assets*, the various stocks would appear thus—

Stocks on hand—

	£	£
Raw Materials	4,000	
Work in Progress	5,500	
Finished Goods	15,000	
		24,500

Some manufacturing concerns wish to know to what extent the gross profit is made up by efficiencies and economies in manufacture and to what extent by efficiencies and economies in the Trading Department. This can be discovered by crediting the Manufacturing Account and debiting the Trading Account, not with the cost of production, but *with the market price of the cost of production* (i.e. the price at which the Trading Department would have to pay if it bought such goods from an outside manufacturer). This would result in a profit on manufacture if the goods were produced cheaper than they could be bought outside. Such profit would be transferred to the credit of Profit and Loss Account, leaving only the true trading profit to appear in the Trading Account, that is, the profit made on buying and selling, which in its turn will be transferred to the credit of the Profit and Loss Account. Losses on manufacturing would, of course, be debited to the Profit and Loss Account.

This use of the market price of manufactured goods rather than the cost price enables the management properly to apportion praise and blame between the Factory or Works Manager on the one hand and the Sales and Advertising Departments on the other hand.

Example

MANUFACTURING AND TRADING AND PROFIT AND LOSS ACCOUNTS
FOR THE YEAR ENDED 31ST DECEMBER, 19..

	£		£
To Stock of Raw Materials, 1st Jan	5,000	By Work in Progress 31st Dec	5,500
,, Purchases of Raw Materials	40,000	,, Cost of Manufactured Goods . . . c/d	85,500
	45,000		
Less Stock, 31st Dec	4,000		
,, Materials consumed	41,000		
,, Work in Progress, 1st Jan	3,000		
,, Wages	35,000		
,, Factory Expenses	12,000		
	£91,000		£91,000
To Cost of Manufactured Goods b/d	85,500	By Market Value of Goods Manufactured (transferred to Trading Account)	98,000
,, Gross Profit on Manufacture transferred to Profit and Loss Account	12,500		
	£98,000		£98,000
To Stock of Finished Goods, 1st Jan	8,000	By Sales (*less* returns)	145,000
,, Market Value of Goods Manufactured transferred from Manufacturing Account	98,000	,, Stock, 31st Dec	7,500
,, Trading Expenses	10,000		
,, Gross Profit c/d	36,500		
	£152,500		£152,500
To Salaries	9,500	By Gross Profit on Trading b/d	36,500
,, Carriage Outwards	500	,, Gross Profit on Manufacture . . . b/d	12,500
,, Heating and Lighting	250		
,, Rent and Rates	1,500		49,000
,, General Expenses	12,000		
,, Discounts Allowed	250	,, Discounts Received	400
,, Net Profit	25,400		
	£49,400		£49,400

EXERCISE 1

What is the purpose of drawing up a Manufacturing Account?

EXERCISE 2

State the advantages of transferring goods manufactured to the Trading Account at current market price rather than at cost price.

EXERCISE 3

From the following information extracted from the books of Waghorn, Ltd., prepare the Manufacturing, Trading and Profit and Loss Accounts for the year ended 31st December, 19..

	£
Sales	140,000
Stock of Raw Materials, 31st Dec.	7,500
Factory Expenses	7,000
Stock of Finished Goods, 1st Jan.	9,000
Work in Progress, 1st Jan.	10,000
Rent Received	100
Warehouse Wages	5,000
General Expenses	9,000
Warehouse Expenses	3,000
Salaries	3,000
Stock of Finished Goods, 31st Dec.	7,000
Carriage Outwards	220
Manufacturing Wages	40,000
Purchases of Raw Materials	55,000
Discounts Received	320
Raw Materials returned	500
Stock of Raw Materials, 1st Jan.	6,000
Rates	1,000
Work in Progress, 31st Dec.	4,000

(Gross Profit £24,000. Net Profit £11,200.)

EXERCISE 4

From the following balances extracted from the books of the Acme Manufacturing Co., Ltd., prepare accounts in a form to disclose—

(i) Cost of manufactured goods sold.
(ii) Cost of production.
(iii) Cost of raw materials consumed.
(iv) Gross profit on manufacture.
(v) Gross profit on sales.
(vi) Net profit.
(vii) Net profit as percentage of sales.
(viii) Gross trading profit as a percentage of sales.

	£
Work in Progress, 1st Jan.	5,000
Manufacturing Wages	20,800
Office Rent and Rates	910
Stock of Raw Materials, 1st Jan.	8,500
Sales	98,000
Carriage on Raw Materials	280
General Expenses	4,500
Carriage Outwards	450
Discounts Allowed	400
Discounts Received	560
Stock of Finished Goods, 1st Jan.	6,000

Depreciation of Factory Machinery	900
Purchases of Raw Materials	30,000
Sales Returns	2,000
Factory Expenses	8,000
Stock of Raw Materials, 31st Dec.	6,500
Work in Progress, 31st Dec.	6,980
Selling Expenses	9,000
Stock of Finished Goods, 31st Dec.	8,000
Office Salaries	5,300

Note—

Goods manufactured are to be transferred to the Sales Department at the current market value, £65,000.

Depreciation of Machinery is to be charged to the Manufacturing Account.

Profit on manufacture, £5,000. Gross profit, £24,000. Net profit, £18,000. Cost of raw materials consumed, £32,000. Cost of production, £60,000. Cost of manufactured goods sold, £63,000. Percentage gross trading profit on sales, 25 per cent. Percentage net profit on sales, 18·75 per cent.

CHAPTER II

BILLS OF EXCHANGE: DEFINITION, DAYS OF GRACE, STAMP DUTIES, ACCEPTANCE, ENDORSEMENT, DISHONOURED BILLS, NOTING, RENEWING, RETIRING. PROMISSORY NOTES

IF cash was demanded from every purchaser in business many transactions would not take place at all. Being granted a reasonable period of credit, the buyer has time in which to dispose of a part or the whole of the goods and so obtain the means to pay. But the trader desires immediate or, at least, early payment. The use of a bill of exchange permits the purchaser to defer payment, and, if necessary, the seller to receive cash at once. It also provides definite evidence that the debtor owes the money. Take the following transaction—

1st January, B. Flint buys £500 goods from P. Coles on credit, to be settled by a two months' bill of exchange.

P. Coles, to whom the £500 is owed, draws up the bill in the following terms—

£500	LONDON,

(1p. Stamp.)

1st January, 19..

TWO MONTHS after date pay to me or my order the sum of *Five hundred pounds* value received.

(Sgd.) *P. Coles*

To *B. Flint*,
108 *Wells Street*,
London.

Coles sends the draft to Flint for "acceptance." Flint signs his name across the face of the bill and adds the word

"Accepted." He thereby assents to be bound by the terms of the bill. The bill is then returned to Coles. The latter has now a valuable document recognized by the law of the land. He may do one of three things with it. (1) He may retain it until the due date and then present it to Flint for payment. (2) Sell it for cash at any time before the due date, and the new holder will present it to Flint for payment. (3) Transfer it to a creditor in payment of his (Coles's) debt.

No. 2 is called "discounting" the bill, and this is usually done with the firm's bankers. A charge is made by the bank calculated at the current market rate of discount on the unexpired term of the bill. This charge, of course, represents a loss to Coles, but he prefers a slightly smaller sum now rather than wait two months for the full amount. The bank presents the bill to Flint in two months' time for payment, receiving the full amount.

Definition

Bills of exchange and cheques are governed by the Bills of Exchange Act, 1882, which defines a bill as—

> An unconditional order in writing, addressed by one person to another, signed by the person giving it, requiring the person to whom it is addressed to pay on demand or at a fixed or determinable future time a sum certain in money to or to the order of a specified person or to bearer.

There are Inland Bills and Foreign Bills, but we are concerned only with the former, which are distinguished by being drawn and payable within the British Isles.

The persons concerned with the bill—the parties to it—are—

The Drawer—who signs the bill ordering the debtor to pay.

The Drawee—the person to whom the bill is addressed and is the debtor.

The Payee—the person to whom the bill is made payable, who may also be the drawer.

Days of Grace

Bills may be payable on demand or at some future date. In the latter case the bill is payable on the third day after the expiration of the term mentioned on it. These extra three days are called "Days of Grace." For example, the bill shown on p. 9 is payable on 4th March. Should the final day for payment fall on a Sunday, Christmas Day, or Good Friday, it is payable on the preceding business day. Should it fall on a Bank Holiday other than Christmas Day or Good Friday, it is payable on the succeeding business day.

Stamp Duties

Bills of exchange must be stamped. This is a means of revenue to the State. The stamp duty on any bill of exchange—whether payable on demand or at a future date—is 1p.

Acceptance

To show his willingness to be bound by the order the drawee must signify his assent to it. His signature alone is sufficient, but the word "accepted" is usually added. The bill may be "domiciled," that is, the acceptor may indicate in his acceptance the place of payment by adding, for example, the name and address of his bank.

The drawer may refuse to take an acceptance which contains any words varying the terms of the bill. If he does not refuse it he is bound by the altered conditions.

Endorsement

The drawer may transfer the bill to a third party as mentioned above. This is called negotiating the bill. If made payable "to————or order" the bill must be endorsed by the drawer by his signing his name across the back of it. Bills drawn payable "to————or bearer" do not require endorsement. If a bill is transferred and the new holder himself transfers it, he is usually required to endorse the bill. The first endorser is always the payee.

Dishonoured Bills

If payment is refused when the bill is presented on the due date it is said to be "dishonoured by non-payment." The holder of the bill should then give notice to all the other parties to the bill, as he has the right to look to any of them for payment. If he obtains payment from the person who endorsed the bill over to him, then that person in turn may press any remaining party for payment, and this may continue until the drawer is reached. He then must turn to the acceptor, and, if necessary, sue him on the dishonoured bill.

Noting a Bill

If proof is required that the bill was duly presented and was dishonoured, it is usual to obtain the services of a Notary Public, who presents the bill a second time and attaches to it a ticket bearing his name, his charges, and the reason for the dishonour. His charges are referred to as noting expenses, and are recoverable from the acceptor in addition to the sum due under the bill.

Renewing a Bill

It is sometimes arranged that the acceptor may give a new bill for a further period instead of cash when the old bill is due for payment. This is termed renewing a bill, and interest is generally added to the fresh bill to compensate the holder for waiting the further period.

Retiring a Bill

An acceptor may approach the holder of a bill for permission to pay before the due date. A bill taken out of circulation in this way is said to be retired. Usually the holder allows the acceptor a "rebate" or "discount" for paying before the expiration of the term.

Promissory Notes

A means of payment akin to the bill of exchange is the promissory note. It is used mainly in load transactions. Whereas the person to whom the debt is owed draws up the bill of exchange, the debtor himself draws up the promissory note. The bill of exchange is an *order* to the debtor to pay. The promissory note is a *promise* by the debtor to pay.

The legal definition is—

An unconditional promise in writing, made by one person to another, signed by the maker, engaging to pay on demand, or at a fixed or determinable future time, a sum certain in money to or to the order of a specified person, or to bearer.

Had a promissory note been given in the above transaction it would have been worded as follows—

£500   LONDON,

(1p. Stamp.)   1st January, 19..

TWO MONTHS after date I promise to pay P. Coles or order the sum of Five hundred pounds value received.

(Sgd.) B. Flint

The stamp duty is 1p. for all promissory notes. Promissory notes do not require acceptance, but the three days of grace apply as for bills of exchange.

The book-keeping entries for promissory notes are similar to those required for bills of exchange and these are explained in the two succeeding chapters.

CHAPTER III

BILLS RECEIVABLE, DISCOUNTING A BILL, PAYMENT ON MATURITY, AND DISHONOURED BILLS

THE book-keeping required is not difficult to grasp once the nature and use of bills is thoroughly understood. First of all it is necessary to point out that a bill of exchange is regarded and termed a bill receivable by the person who should receive the sum due on it, and as a bill payable by the person who has to pay it. Secondly, a debtor, by giving a bill, in effect pays his debt and the bill takes the place of the book debt as an asset in the accounts of the receiver.

Bills Receivable

Examples

July   1. Sold £200 goods to B. Kennedy and drew a bill on him for two months, which he accepted.
Discounted this bill with my bankers; discount charges, £22.

       7. Sold £150 goods to R. Durnford and received from him his acceptance for one month for that amount.

      8. W. Beaumont, who owed me £300 for goods supplied, accepted the bill I drew on him for two months.

Aug. 10. R. Durnford's bill, paid into bank for collection, was duly met at maturity.

Sept. 8. Paid W. Beaumont's bill into bank for collection.

    11. W. Beaumont's bill returned dishonoured; noting charges £0·37.

The usual entries will be made in the books for the sale of goods to these customers, so that £200 will appear to the debit of B. Kennedy, £150 to the debit of R. Durnford, and £300 on the debit side of W. Beaumont's account. In each case I wrote out the bill and sent it to the debtor for his accept-ance. He returned it duly accepted. On my receiving the accepted bill the book-keeping entries begin. The debtor gives the acceptance; I receive it. The rules are, therefore—

Credit the debtor's Personal Account in the Sales Ledger.

Debit Bills Receivable Account in the General Ledger.

The latter is a new real account opened to record the bills receivable in my possession. Should I prepare a Balance Sheet before the bills are discounted or paid at maturity, the balance of the Bills Receivable Account will appear among the current assets.

Discounting a Bill

I decided to discount B. Kennedy's bill with my bankers. This was a sale to them of the bill at something less than its face value. The bill is handed over to the bank, who place to my account the full amount. On examining my pass book I subsequently find that they have withdrawn from my account £2 for discounting charges.

The entries on discounting are—

Credit Bills Receivable Account.

Debit Bank Account (in the Cash Book) with the full amount of the bill.

And for the discount charges, as these represent a loss to me—

Credit Bank Account (in the Cash Book).

Debit Discount on Bills Account (in the General Ledger).

On closing the books the balance of the Discount on Bills Account is transferred to the debit of Profit and Loss Account.

Payment on Maturity

I decided to retain R. Durnford's bill until due for payment on 10th August. It is usual to hand over a bill to one's bankers two or three days before the due date for them to present it for payment to the acceptor's bankers. This is "paying the bill into bank for collection," and as the bill is given over to the bank and it is assumed that the bill will be paid in due course, the following entries are then made—

Credit Bills Receivable Account;

Debit Bank Account (in the Cash Book);

and if the bill is met no further entries are required.

Dishonoured Bills

I decided also to retain W. Beaumont's bill until maturity and paid it into bank for collection, making the entries in the Bills Receivable Account and the Bank Account as explained above. My bank, however, notified me that payment was refused and that they have charged me with £0·37 for noting expenses. The entry on the debit side of Bank Account must be cancelled by an entry of a similar sum on the credit side, and an entry must be made of the £0·37 charged to my account. The dishonoured bill is valueless except as evidence of the debt due. The personal debt of W. Beaumont to me is revived. The entries required are—

Credit Bank Account (in the Cash Book) with the amount of the bill and the noting expenses.

Debit the debtor's account (in this case, W. Beaumont) with the total of the bill *and* the noting expenses.

Once again W. Beaumont is my debtor and I shall take steps to ascertain his intention as regards payment.

Had I discounted the bill with my bankers and it had been dishonoured at maturity, the bank would have looked to me for reimbursement, and exactly similar entries would have been required.

These examples are worked below, and the above rules may be traced through the accounts. The debit entries only for the original sale transactions are shown.

SALES LEDGER

Dr.					B. Kennedy (7)			Cr.
19.. Jul. 1	To Goods	.	SJ	£ 200·00	19.. Jul. 1	By Bill Receivable	GL.40	£ 200.00

Dr.   R. DURNFORD (20)   *Cr.*

19.. Jul. 7	To Goods	SJ	£ 150·00	19.. Jul. 7	By Bill Receivable	GL.40	£ 150·00

Dr.   W. BEAUMONT (25)   *Cr.*

19..
Jul. 8
Sep. 11
	To Goods .
	,, Dishonoured
	  Bill and
	  Noting
	     Charges .
		SJ
		
		CB
			£
			300·00
			
			300·37
				19..
				Jul. 8
					By Bills Receivable	GL.40	£
							300·00

GENERAL LEDGER

Dr.   BILLS RECEIVABLE (40)   *Cr.*

19..
Jul. 1
7
8
	To B. Kennedy
	,, R. Durnford .
	,, W. Beaumont .
		SL. 7
		SL.20
		SL.25
			£
			200·00
			150·00
			300·00
				19..
				Jul. 1
				
				Aug. 10
				
				Sep. 8
					By Bank
					  (Kennedy's
					  Bill
					   Discounted)
					,, Bank
					  (R. Durn-
					   ford's Bill) .
					,, Bank
					  (W. Beau-
					   mont's Bill) .
						
						CB
						
						CB
						
						CB
							£
							
							200·00
							
							150·00
							
							300·00

Dr.   DISCOUNT ON BILLS (56)   *Cr.*

19..
Jul. 1
	To Bank
	  (Kennedy's
	  Bill) .
		CB	£
			
			2·00
							£

CASH BOOK (BANK COLUMNS ONLY ARE SHOWN)

19..
Jul. 1
 	
Aug. 10
 	
Sep. 8
	To Bill Receivable
	  (Kennedy's
	  Bill
	   Discounted) .
	,, Bill Receivable
	  (R. Durn-
	   ford's Bill
	   Paid) .
	,, Bill Receivable
	  (W. Beau-
	   mont's Bill)
		
		GL.40
		
		GL.40
		
		GL.40
			£
			
			200·00
			
			150·00
			
			300·00
				19..
				Jul. 1
				
				Sep. 11
					By Discount on
					  Bill
					  (B. Kennedy)
					,, Dishonoured
					  Bill
					  (W. Beau-
					   mont) .
					,, Noting Charges
						GL.56
						
						SL.25
						SL.25
							£
							2·00
							
							300·00
							0·37

EXERCISE 5

On 1st September, 19.., J. Hill, of Hide Lane, London, E.C.3, drew a bill on E. J. Paine, of Austin Road, Manchester, for £320 payable in three months. Draw the bill and state the due date.

EXERCISE 6

M. Rendell sold goods to L. Scott on 5th August to the value of £220. On that day M. Rendell drew a bill on L. Scott for the amount at three months. L. Scott accepted the bill, which was duly met at maturity.

Record these transactions in M. Rendell's books.

EXERCISE 7

C. Warren supplied L. Standford on 15th May with goods valued at £600. On that day Standford forwarded his acceptance for two months for the amount owing. The bill was duly met on maturity.

Record these matters in C. Warren's books.

EXERCISE 8

On 1st July T. G. Brown bought £430 goods from J. Smith & Co. and gave them his acceptance for the amount for three months. J. Smith & Co. at once discounted the bill with their bankers who charged £6 discount

Record these transactions in J. Smith & Co.'s books.

EXERCISE 9

G. Spencer is in business as a hardware merchant. On 1st December his position was as follows—

					£
Cash in hand	.	.	.	.	54·52
Cash at bank	.	.	.	.	432·00
Stock	.	.	.	.	1,500·00

Open his books and record the following transactions—

		£
Dec. 1.	Sold to J. Thompson & Sons sundry gardening tools .	58·00
3.	Sold to Harding & Hobson, goods . . .	212·50
4.	Received from Harding & Hobson their acceptance for one month for the amount of their amount.	
9.	Bought from the Star Manufacturing Co., Ltd., lathes	300·00
14.	Paid sundry expenses in cash	6·17
18.	Sold to J. Thompson & Sons, goods. . . .	42·00
20.	Drew on J. Thompson & Sons for the amount of their account at two months and received bill duly accepted.	

£

Dec. 20. Discounted with bankers J. Thompson & Sons' accept-
           ance. Discount charges   .   .   .   .   .   1·25
     28. Paid salaries by cheque .   .   .   .   .   .   60·00
     30. Paid the Star Manufacturing Co., Ltd., their account by
           cheque, *less* 5 per cent cash discount.
Extract Trial Balance as at 31st December.
                    (Trial Balance totals, £2,314·02.)
Prepare final accounts as at 31st December. Stock on hand, £1,640. (Gross
Profit, £152·50. Net Profit, £100·08. Balance Sheet totals, £2,086·60.)

EXERCISE 10

On 10th March P. Coles owed E. Andrews £200 for goods supplied, and on
that date accepted a bill of exchange at three months for the amount. On 12th
March E. Andrews discounted the bill with his bankers, who charged £2·75.
On the due date Coles dishonoured the bill. Make the entries necessary to
record these transactions in the books of E. Andrews.

CHAPTER IV

BILLS PAYABLE, PAYMENT ON PRESENTATION, AND BILL BOOKS

A BILL of exchange is regarded as a bill payable by the person who has eventually to pay it. The entries required differ from those for bills receivable, for whereas the latter is received from a debtor, the bill payable is given to a creditor.

Example

I owed W. Goodwin £80 for goods supplied during December. On 1st January I forwarded to him my acceptance for three months. I arrange with my banker to meet the bill on presentation.

Goodwin, my creditor, draws the bill on me and I return it to him accepted.

The entries necessary are—

Debit the Creditor's (Goodwin's) Account in the Bought Ledger as he receives the bill.

Credit Bills Payable Account in the General Ledger, as I give the bill.

These entries have the effect of closing W. Goodwin's account and opening a new liability account called the Bills Payable Account. The bill will be presented to me on maturity, and I shall pay it, but as Goodwin may discount the bill I cannot tell in advance who will be the final holder. The Bills Payable Account represents a liability due to unknown holders of bills accepted by me.

Payment on Presentation

I know the due dates of the bills outstanding and take care that my account has a large enough balance to meet them. I arrange with the bank to pay such bills on presentation. The bank will take the amount from my account and I shall receive back the bill, which may then be cancelled or destroyed.

The entries required on payment are—

Credit Bank Account (in the Cash Book).

Debit Bills Payable Account.

Should the Bills Payable Account show a balance representing unpaid bills when the final accounts are prepared, such a balance must appear among the current liabilities in the Balance Sheet.

The accounts affected in the above example will appear as below—

BOUGHT LEDGER

Dr.　　　　　　　　　　　W. Goodwin (24)　　　　　　　　　*Cr.*

19.. Jan. 1	To Bills Payable	GL.7	£ 80	19.. Jan. 1	By Balance .	b/d	£ 80

GENERAL LEDGER

Dr.　　　　　　　　　　　Bills Payable (7)　　　　　　　　　*Cr.*

19.. Apr. 4	To Bank .	CB	£ 80	19.. Jan. 1	By W. Goodwin .	BL.24	£ 80

CASH BOOK

Dr.　　　　　　　(Bank Columns Only are Shown)　　　　　　*Cr.*

			£	19.. Apr. 4	By Bills Payable (W. Goodwin)	GL.7	£ 80

Bills Books

If bill transactions are few in number, the original entry is made in the Journal Proper and posted therefrom to the Ledgers. In practice, when bill transactions are sufficiently numerous to warrant them, Bills Books are introduced. Details of the bills are entered into the Bills Books and posted to the appropriate personal accounts in the Sales and Bought Ledgers. Periodically the totals of the Bills Receivable Book and the Bills Payable Book are posted respectively to the Bills Receivable Account and Bills Payable Account in the General

BILLS RECEIVABLE BOOK

No.	Date	Bill to be Credited to	Led. Fol.	Amount	Date of Bill	Term	Due Date	Drawer	Acceptor	Where Payable	Remarks
1	19.. July 1	B. Kennedy	7	£ 200	19.. July 1	2 mo.	19.. Sept. 4	Self	B. Kennedy	Barclays	Discounted with Bank, 1st July, 19... Paid, 10th August, 19...
2	7	R. Durnford	20	150	7	1 mo.	Aug. 10	Self	R. Durnford		
3	8	W. Beaumont	25	300	8	2 mo.	Sept. 11	Self	W. Beaumont		Dishonoured, 11th September, 19...

BILLS PAYABLE BOOK

No.	Date	Bill to be Debited to	Led. Fol.	Amount	Date of Bill	Term	Due Date	Drawer	Where Payable	Remarks
1	19.. Jan. 1	W. Goodwin	24	£ 80	19.. Jan. 1	3 mo.	19.. Apr. 4	W. Goodwin	London	Paid at maturity

Ledger. The double-entry remains, of course, in the Ledgers, namely, in the Personal Accounts and the Bills Accounts, but, in the case of bills receivable, the debit entries in the Bills Receivable Account are the periodical totals from the Bills Book; similarly, for bills payable the credit entries are the periodical totals from the Bills Payable Book. These totals are posted from the Bills Book monthly, quarterly, or at the end of the accounting period.

Just as the Purchases Journal and Sales Journal provide a separate classified record and permit of the entries being made more expeditiously, so the Bills Books yield similar advantages in the case of bills, and, at the same time, avoid the overloading of the Bills Accounts with details.

Various rulings are in use, but the specimen rulings given on p. 22 will convey to the reader the kind of information that is recorded. So many columns may make the book appear somewhat complicated, but it should be borne in mind that a few only contain the information required for the double-entry book-keeping; the remaining columns are simply for record purposes.

The essential columns are—

1. The date of the bill.
2. The amount of the bill.
3. In Bills Receivable Book, the person to be credited; in Bills Payable Book, the person to be debited.
4. The term and due date of the bill.

EXERCISE 11

Thomas Jones bought goods, £500, on 1st June from London Stores, Ltd., and gave them his acceptance for two months. He arranged for his bankers to meet the bill, which was duly presented on maturity.

Record these transactions in the books of T. Jones.

EXERCISE 12

On 4th January G. Kelly owed J. Hopkins £650 for goods supplied, and on that date accepted a bill drawn on him by J. Hopkins at three months. The bill was duly paid on presentation to G. Kelly's bankers at maturity.

Make the necessary entries in G. Kelly's books.

EXERCISE 13

G. Spencer, in business as a hardware merchant, finds his position on 1st January as follows—

		£
Cash in hand	. . . . . .	48·35
Cash at bank	. . . . . .	185·75
Stock	. . . . .	1,640·00
Bill receivable (Harding & Hobson due 7th January)	. . . . .	212·50

Open his books and enter the following transactions—

		£
Jan. 2.	Bought drilling machines from the Star Manufacturing Co., Ltd., and forwarded them acceptance for one month for the amount	300·00
4.	Sold goods for cash	104·00
7.	Sold job line of wire netting and received cheque .	84·00
7.	Paid into bank for collection Harding & Hobson's bill, which was duly met.	
12.	Sold to J. Thompson & Sons, goods . . .	160·00
14.	Bought from Lane & Sons, saws and chisels . .	60·00
17.	Accepted Lane & Sons' bill for three months for the amount of their account.	
18.	Received from J. Thompson & Sons accepted bill of exchange for two months	160·00
24.	Cash sales	224·50
25.	Paid cash into bank	300·00
28.	Paid salaries by cheque	60·00
29.	Paid sundry expenses in cash	4·62
Feb. 3.	Purchased for cash, goods	20·00
5.	Bill payable (Star Manufacturing Co., Ltd.) due this day paid by bank.	

Take out Trial Balance.

(Trial Balance totals, £2,719·10.)

Prepare final accounts as at 6th February. Stock on hand, £1,660. (Gross Profit, £212·50. Net Profit, £147·88. Balance Sheet totals, £2294·48.)

EXERCISE 14

George McArthur is in business as a jeweller and cutler. On 31st December, 19.., his financial position was as follows—

			£
Sundry Debtors:	L. Pirrie	. . . . .	84·38
	V. Fleet	. . . .	48·00

	£
Stock	648·37
Cash at bank	409·23
Cash in hand	10·30
Furniture and fittings	226·40
Creditor: D. Perkins	302·52
Bill payable (L. Kirk)	100·00

Open the accounts necessary to record the above particulars in the Ledger, and post thereto, through the proper subsidiary books, the following transactions—

19..
Jan. 2. Drew by cheque from bank £50 for office purposes.
    4. Paid in cash wages and office expenses, £18·23.
    5. Received from V. Fleet cheque in settlement of his account *less* 5 per cent cash discount. Paid same into bank.
    8. Cash sales since 2nd January, paid into bank, £101·43.
    12. Bill payable (L. Kirk) due this day was duly met by bank.
    17. Purchased on credit from D. Dennison—
        24 safety razors at £0·25 each.
        12 doz. table knives at £1·60 per doz.
        2 plated tea and coffee sets at £8·40 per set. The whole invoice subject to 10 per cent trade discount.
    20. Sold, on credit to L. Pirrie—
        3 doz. pairs of scissors at 10p. per pair.
        24 table forks at £1·90 per doz.
    21. Returned as defective to D. Dennison 5 safety razors supplied on the 17th inst.
    22. McArthur drew £50 from the bank for private purposes.
    23. Paid D. Perkins by cheque, £202·52, and accepted a bill at three months for the balance of his account.
    23. Paid in cash wages and office expenses, £18·32, and purchased for cash, stationery, £3·38.
    31. Purchased by cheque new typewriter, £21.

Balance the Ledgers, bring down the balances, and extract a Trial Balance as on 31st January, 19...

N.B. No Profit and Loss Account or Balance Sheet is to be prepared.

(Trial Balance totals, £1,270·79.)

(*R.S.A.*)

EXERCISE 15

C. Testout is a stationer and fancy goods merchant. On 1st May, 19.., his books revealed the following position—

	£
Fixtures and fittings	340·30
Stock in trade	1,871·62
Sundry Debtors: R. Ink	34·25
C. Foil	7·50

	£
Creditor: P. Card	140·80
Bill payable (J. Towers)	150·00
Cash at bank	54·41

Open the accounts necessary to record the above position in the Ledgers and post thereto, through the proper subsidiary books, the following transactions—

19..

May 2. Withdrew £50 from the bank for office purposes.

   6. R. Ink settled his account, *less* 5 per cent cash discount. Paid the amount into the bank.

  10. Cash sales to date, £160·07. Paid same into bank.

  14. Bill payable (J. Towers) due this day duly met by the bank.

  18. Purchased, on credit, from the Stationery Association, Ltd.—
    200 boxes of envelopes at £0·22 per box.
    30 reams white foolscap at £0·57 per ream.
    6 doz. fancy blotting pads at £0·67 per doz. The whole invoice subject to a trade discount of 10 per cent.

  20. Paid, in cash, rates on premises to Lady Day, £26·75.

  22. Goods sold for cash (and included in cash sales on the 10th inst.) were returned, and a cheque was sent to customer for £3, being the value of the goods.

  24. Sold, on credit, to C. Foil—
    4 reams blotting paper at £0·77 per ream.
    4 gross pens at £0·57 per gross.
    8 bottles of ink at £0·46 per bottle.
    2 cases of fancy leather goods at £7·50 per case. Trade discount of 20 per cent on the leather goods and 10 per cent on the other goods was allowed.

  27. Purchased a job lot of books for £10 and paid for same in cash.

  29. C. Foil returned one case of leather goods supplied on the 24th inst. Sent him credit note for the value of the goods as invoiced.

  31. Paid all office cash into bank.

Balance the Ledgers, bring down the balances, and extract a Trial Balance as at 31st May, 19...

N.B. No Profit and Loss Account or Balance Sheet is to be prepared.
    (Trial Balance totals, £2,396·90.)

                (R.S.A.)

EXERCISE 16

John Owen is a wholesale grocer and provision merchant. On 1st January 19.., his books revealed the following position—

	£
Stock	625·50
Fixtures and fittings	171·00
Sundry Debtors: L. Kirk	26·41
R. Clay	74·52

					£
Creditor: J. Barnett	.	.	.	.	184·38
Cash at bank	.	.	.	.	342·38
Bill receivable (S. Clark)	.	.	.	.	150·00

Open the accounts necessary to record the above state of affairs and post thereto, through the proper subsidiary books, the following transactions—

19..
Jan. 1. Drew from the bank, for office purposes, £60.

2. Paid, in cash: wages, £22·50; fire insurance premiums, £8·50.

3. Cash sales to date, £104·36. Paid same into bank.

7. Received from L. Kirk, cheque in settlement of his account. Paid the amount into bank.

10. Sent to L. Kirk, cash, £1·00 for discount allowed him on settlement of his account.

13. Bought, on credit, from the Grocers' Supply Co.—
   ½ doz. hams, total weight 1¼ cwt., at £20·65 per cwt.
   1½ doz. tinned fruits at £0·60 per doz.
   7 cwt. sugar at £3·00 per cwt.
   1 chest tea for £32·75. The whole invoice subject to a trade discount of 10 per cent.

15. Sold, on credit, to R. Clay—
   3 gross tins condensed milk at £9·00 per gross, subject to a trade discount of 20 per cent.
   28 lb. dried fruit at 20p. per lb.
   24 tins biscuits at £0·60 per tin.

20. Returned to the Grocers' Supply Co. the chest of tea supplied on the 13th inst. as unsaleable. They agreed to allow credit for the price as invoiced.

22. Bill receivable (S. Clark) due this day was collected by the bank.

24. Paid the Grocers' Supply Co. their account (*less* 2½ per cent cash discount) by cheque.

27. Accepted bill of exchange, drawn by J. Barnett, for the amount due to him.

Balance the Ledger, bring down the balances, and extract a Trial Balance as on 31st January, 19...

N.B. No Profit and Loss Account or Balance Sheet is to be prepared.

(Trial Balance totals, £1,2566·31.)

(*R.S.A.*)

EXERCISE 17

J. Litchfield carries on the business of a boot and shoe warehouseman. On 1st May, 19.., his books revealed the following position—

					£
Premises .	.	.	.	.	7,800·00
Office furniture and equipment .	.	.	.	.	774·75

						£
Stock-in-trade	.	.	.	.	.	2,480·00
Cash in hand	.	.	.	.	.	154·00
Bank overdraft	.	.	.	.	.	84·00
Sundry Debtors: T. Linder	.	.	.	.	506·75
E. Bradley	.	.	.	.	454·50
Creditor: J. Bernstein	.	.	.	.	1,569·85

Open the accounts necessary to record the above position in the books of J. Litchfield and post thereto, through the proper subsidiary books, the following transactions—

19..

May 1. Paid into bank £100 of the cash in hand.

   4. Sold to E. Bradley on credit—
      100 pairs men's shoes at £1·50 per pair.
      15 doz. pairs ladies' Russian boots at £2·10 per pair. The whole invoice subject to a trade discount of 10 per cent.

   5. Paid by cheque insurance premium of 1 per cent on value of stock in trade as at 1st May, 19...

   6. Paid wages, in cash, £10·60.

   7. Purchased, for cash, a job lot of men's heavy boots, £28.

  10. E. Bradley returned 10 pairs men's shoes supplied on 4th May as unsuitable, and for which credit note was sent.

  11. Bought, on credit, from J. Bernstein—
      4 doz. pairs ladies' dance shoes at £1·90 per pair.
      12 doz. pairs children's bathing shoes at £3·00 per dozen pairs.
      Case of boot polish for £4·25.
      Packing and non-returnable crate invoiced at £0·60.

  12. T. Linder settled his account by cheque, *less* 5 per cent cash discount. Paid cheque into bank.

  13. Exchanged office typewriter for new machine, paying by cheque cash adjustment of £35.

  14. Gave J. Bernstein a bill at three months for £1,000 on account.

  14. J. Litchfield brought £500 additional capital into the business, which was paid into bank.

Balance the Ledger, bring down the balances, and extract a Trial Balance as on 14th May, 19...

N.B. No Profit and Loss Account or Balance Sheet is to be prepared.

(Trial Balance totals, £13,193·25.)

(*R.S.A.*)

CHAPTER V

CONSIGNMENT ACCOUNTS

TRADE between different places in the country and between different countries may take place by way of consignments to agents who undertake to sell the goods on commission. The principal forwarding the goods is known as the consignor, the agent receiving the goods being the consignee. Though the goods are sent to the consignee they do not represent a sale to him. He holds them only as agent for the consignor and for sale on the consignor's behalf. The consignor may forward to the agent a *pro forma* invoice containing a description of the goods, quantity or weight, shipping marks and other details. The purpose of the invoice is to give to the consignee in concise form all relevant information regarding the consignment and to indicate the minimum selling price. It does not charge the consignee with the value of the goods.

When the consignee sells the goods, he collects the proceeds and, after deducting his expenses and commission, remits the net amount to the consignor. The commission is usually calculated as a percentage of the gross proceeds and should the consignee guarantee the consignor against loss from bad debts, he is paid an additional percentage, called a *del credere* commission. The consignee renders to the consignor a statement called an Account Sales containing particulars of the consignment, the gross price obtained, his expenses and commission and showing finally the net amount due to the consignor. The consignor treats the goods he sends to the consignee as a Consignment Outwards; to the consignee it is a Consignment Inwards.

Consignment Outwards

Example

S. Singleton, of London, consigned 12 cases of fancy goods to H. Meerat, of Karachi, on 15th July, paying for freight, insurance, etc., £50. The goods were valued at £1,000, cost price. On 20th September Singleton received from the consignee his Account Sales showing gross proceeds £1,600, landing charges, dock dues and duty paid £80, and his commission at 5 per cent + 1¼ per cent *del credere*. On the same day a banker's draft on London was received from the consignee for the net proceeds.

Show the necessary entries in the consignor's books.

As the movement of the goods does not represent a sale to Meerat, no entry can be made in the Sales Day Book or Sales Account nor can Meerat's personal account be debited with the value of the goods consigned. Instead, two accounts are opened, a "Consignment Outwards Account" and a "Consignment to H. Meerat Account," the former to record that goods have left the warehouse on consignment and the latter to record that Meerat has received goods on consignment, the entries being at cost price.

The sequence of entries is as follows—

1. Open a "Consignment to H Meerat Account" and *debit* to it the value at cost price of the goods consigned to him.

2. Open a "Consignment Outwards Account" and *credit* to it the value at cost price of the goods consigned.

3. *Debit* all shipping charges and other expenses relating to the consignment to "Consignment to H. Meerat Account." *Credit* all such charges and expenses to Cash, if paid in cash, or to the creditors' accounts if on credit.

4. On receipt of the Account Sales from the consignee, *credit* the gross proceeds to the Consignment to H. Meerat Account and *debit* that Account with the consignee's expenses and commission as shown on the Account Sales. Open a personal account for H. Meerat if none already exists and *debit* his account with the gross proceeds, *crediting* his expenses and commission. The account will then show on balance the amount of the net proceeds as a debt due from the consignee. On receipt of the net proceeds, make a debit entry to Cash and credit the amount to Meerat's personal account which is thereby closed.

5. Transfer the balance of the Consignment to H. Meerat's

Account to Profit and Loss Account, such balance representing the profit or loss on the venture.

6. Transfer the balance of the Consignments Outwards Account to the Trading Account at the close of the year, showing it as a separate item and not including it in the total sales. The total sales includes the gross profit whereas the above balance is at cost price only and to merge the two would render the total sales figure ineffective for purposes of comparison with the sales figures of previous years.

The following are Ledger accounts showing the appropriate entries—

Dr. CONSIGNMENT OUTWARDS

			£					£
Dec. 31	To Transfer to Trading A/c .		1,000	July 15	By Consignment to H. Meerat .	J		1,000

Dr. CONSIGNMENT TO H. MEERAT, KARACHI *Cr.*

			£			£
Jul. 15	To Consignment Outwards .	J	1,000	Sept. 20	By Consignee, being gross proceeds	1,600
	,, Cash (freight and insurance) .		50			
Sept. 20	,, Consignee Landing charges, etc. .		80			
	5% Commission		80			
	1¼% *del credere*		20			
	,, Profit and Loss A/c .		370			
			£1,600			£1,600

Dr. / H. MEERAT *Cr.*

			£			£
Sept. 20	To Consignment A/c, being gross proceeds .		1,600	Sept. 20	By Consignment A/c— Landing charges, etc. .	
					5% Commission .	80
					1¼% *del credere* .	80
					,, Cash (net proceeds) . .	20
						1,420
			£1,600			£1,600

Bills of Exchange

If the consignee remits by bill of exchange, the consignee's personal account is credited and Bills Receivable Account is debited with the amount of the bill. Subsequent entries will depend upon the consignor's decision either to discount the bill or to keep it until its due date.

In some cases the consignor may arrange to draw on the consignee when shipping the goods. Such a bill is usually drawn for about three-quarters of the value of the goods and for such a period after sight as will give time to the consignee to receive and sell the goods before he has to meet the bill. The consignor attaches the shipping documents to the bill and sells it to his bankers who forward it to their agents to obtain the consignee's acceptance against the handing over of the shipping documents. Such a bill with documents attached is called a documentary bill. The amount of the bill is credited to the consignee's personal account as part payment of the net proceeds and debited to Bills Receivable Account. On the bill being sold to the bank, Bills Receivable Account is credited with the bill and Cash is debited with the actual cash received, the discount charge being debited to Discount on Bills Account.

As the bill is drawn for a part only of the net proceeds there will be a balance due from the consignor. This will be treated in the usual way on receipt of the particulars in the Account Sales and of the remittance.

Consignments and the Balance Sheet

If the final accounts and Balance Sheet have to be prepared and goods are out on consignment, the Consignment to Agent Account will be balanced and closed and the balance carried down for the next trading period. This balance will appear in Balance Sheet on the assets side as Stock on Consignment.

It may happen that part of the goods have been sold and notified by Account Sales. Then the unsold portion must be valued before it can be shown in the Balance Sheet. The consignor's expenses and possibly some part of the consignee's expenses already notified may relate to the whole consignment. These will have to be apportioned between the sold and the unsold portions of the consignment. The value of the unsold portion, including its share of the expenses, is credited to the Consignment to Agent Account and is also carried down to the debit side of the Account for the next financial period. This is the item that will appear in the Balance Sheet as Stock on Consignment. The Consignment to Agent Account is then balanced and the balance, representing the profit or loss on the sold portion of the consignment, is carried to the Profit and Loss Account in the usual way.

Consignments Inwards

The consignee treats the consignment as a Consignment Inwards. The goods are received by him for sale on behalf of the consignor. Their arrival does not involve any entry in his accounts as he is not a debtor to anyone for their value. He will record the description and quantities of the goods in a Consignment Inwards Stock Book for memorandum purposes only. Thereafter he is concerned only with the expenses incurred, the sales which take place, his commission, and the remission of the net proceeds to the consignor.

Example. (The above example reworded from the consignee's point of view.)

> Received on 10th August from S. Singleton, London, on consignment 12 cases of fancy goods. Expenses (landing, dock dues and duty) paid, £80. The goods realized on sale, £1,600. Commission 5 per cent + 1¼ per cent *del credere*.
> Forwarded Account Sales and banker's draft for net proceeds to consignor on 29th August.

The only new account required is a personal account for the consignor, S. Singleton. The entries to record the dealings with the consignment and the proceeds are as follows—

1. *Debit* Consignor's personal Account and *credit* Cash with the expenses paid out.

2. *Debit* customers' personal accounts if goods sold on credit or *debit* Cash if sold for cash; *credit* Consignor's Account with the gross proceeds of sale.

3. Calculate the commission and *debit* the amount to the Consignor's Account, *crediting* Commission Account for a like sum for eventual transfer to Profit and Loss Account.

4. On remitting the net proceeds, *debit* the amount to the Consignor's Account and *credit* Cash or Bills Payable Account as the case may be.

The Consignor's Account is shown below and it will be seen that the entry of the sum remitted to the consignor closes the account, such sum being the balance of the Account after the entry of the expenses, sales, and commission.

Dr.					S. SINGLETON		Cr.
			£				£
Aug. 10	To Cash (Landing charges, etc.)	.	80	Aug. 29	By Sundry Debtors (being proceeds of sale of consignment)	.	
,, 29	,, Commission	.	100				1,600
	,, Cash (Banker's draft for net proceeds)	.	1,420				
			£1,600				£1,600

EXERCISE 18

A London trader consigns goods £500 to South Africa and pays charges and freight £50. His agent informs him that the goods realized £660, and, after deducting charges and commission £48, encloses a cheque for the balance. Enter these transactions in the books of the London trader.

(U.L.C.I.)

EXERCISE 19

On 1st October, Bond & Co., of Liverpool, shipped per the S.S. *Majola* "on consignment" to Perbera & Co., Colombo, goods which were invoiced to them *pro forma* as follows: 20 pieces—30 yds. each (600 yds.) linings at 25p. per yd. The following expenses were paid by Messrs. Bond: packing charges £4·25; marine insurance £0·90, shipping charges and B/L £1·15; freight £4. Under date 5th January, Messrs. Perbera submitted A/S showing the sale of the consignment to have realized £250 gross; and showing deductions for fire insurance 20p., dock dues £0·65., porterage £0·75, commission and *del credere* 4½ per cent (on gross sales), and enclosing demand draft on the Ceylon Bank in settlement of the transaction. Show the whole of the entries which are necessary, including the closing of the Ledger Account in the books of Messrs. Bond & Co. only.

(N.C.T.E.C.)

EXERCISE 20

John Brown consigned a quantity of radio sets to his agent Henry Jones.
On 15th September, Jones sold the consignment for £280 and paid sundry
charges amounting in all to £8·40. On 20th September, Jones sent Brown, two
bills of exchange for £100 each, for 4 and 6 months respectively, and a cheque
for the balance due after deducting the above expenses and 15 per cent commission on the gross proceeds.

The first bill was met on the due date. The second was renewed for a further
6 months, Jones paying interest at the rate of 5 per cent per annum, paid by
cheque.

Set out in Journal entry form the whole of these transactions as they would
appear in John Brown's books.

(*R.S.A.*)

EXERCISE 21

Watson & Co., of London, consigned to Stevenson Bros., of Cape Town,
for sale, goods which cost £1,240 but were invoiced *pro forma* at £1,590.
Watson & Co. paid freight, £83, and insurance, £21. In due course, Stevenson
Bros. sent an Account Sales showing that part of the goods had been sold for
£1,210, and that their charges were £98 plus a commission of 4 per cent on
the gross proceeds. They also sent Watson & Co. a sight draft for the amount
due.

Show the Account Sales and the necessary accounts in Watson & Co.'s
Ledger, noting that the unsold goods were valued at £573.

(*U.E.I.*)

EXERCISE 22

S. Spencer received a consignment of goods from H. Meerat, Karachi,
invoiced *pro forma* at cost £500. Spencer made the following payments on 1st
July: dock charges, £5; carriage £12; duty, £25.

Spencer sold the goods for cash, £750, on 15th July. His commission is 4
per cent of the gross proceeds. Spencer remitted the net proceeds by sight
draft to H. Meerat on 17th July.

Record these entries as they should appear in S. Spencer's books.

EXERCISE 23

Turton & Co., of Sheffield, consigned hardware valued at £85 (invoice
value) to an agent in Calcutta. Carriage, freight, and insurance £62, was paid
by the consignors. The Calcutta agent paid the following expenses: cartage
£1·40; warehousing, £2; town dues £1·25; and sundry expenses, £2·35. He
sold the goods for £1,036, on which amount he was entitled to a commission
of 3¾ per cent. He remitted draft to balance the account. Show by means of
the Journal and the Ledger the entries that would be made in the consignee's
books.

(*N.C.T.E.C.*)

CHAPTER VI

JOINT VENTURES

SOMETIMES two or more businesses decide that they will join together for one particular trading project—or series of projects—and share the profit made. For the occasion they can be regarded as a partnership, though for the rest of their business operations they will continue to trade separately.

If these joint ventures are few in number, there will be no need to keep separate books of account for the temporary partnership. Each adventurer will open a "Joint Venture with ───── Account" and debit it with all moneys spent in furthering the venture, at the same time crediting his Cash Book. He will debit his Cash Book with moneys received in connexion with the venture and credit the Joint Venture Account.

On completion of the venture, each adventurer will send a copy of the account as it appears in his books to his co-adventurer(s). The separate accounts are then combined into a single statement which will show the profit or loss made and its division between the adventurers: this statement is, in fact, the Profit and Loss Account for the venture and does not appear in its entirety, in any of the adventurers' books. It is a Memorandum Account only.

Each adventurer, having agreed his share of profit from the Memorandum Account, will debit his "Joint Venture with ───── Account" with his share of the profit and credit his Profit and Loss Account. If a loss is made, these entries, of course, will be reversed.

The "Joint Venture with ───── Account" will now be left with either a debit or a credit balance. A debit balance will indicate money due *from* the co-adventurer(s): a credit balance will indicate that payment is due *to* the co-adventurer(s). The accounts are then cleared by appropriate payments between the adventurers.

Example

S. Green and D. Grey enter into a joint venture to sell a consignment of goods, sharing profits and losses equally.

Green bought the goods on 5th January, paying £1,500 for them. The following day he received a cheque from Grey for £500. On 8th January Green paid various expenses totalling £28 in connexion with the purchase.

Grey sold two-thirds of the goods for £1,450 on 24th January and Green sold the balance for £650 on 22nd January. Selling expenses were: Green £4; Grey £10. Settlements were made on 31st January.

In Green's Books—

Dr.	JOINT VENTURE WITH D. GREY ACCOUNT				Cr.
		£			£
Jan. 5	To Bank—Purchases	1,500	Jan. 6	By Bank—D. Grey .	50
8	,, Bank—Expenses	28	22	,, Sale of Goods .	650
22	,, Selling Expenses .	4	31	,, Bank—D. Grey .	661
31	,, Share of Profit (to Profit and Loss A/c)	279			
		£1,811			£1,811

In Grey's Books—

Dr.	JOINT VENTURE WITH S. GREEN ACCOUNT				Cr.
		£			£
Jan. 6	To Bank—S. Green .	500	Jan. 24	By Sale of Goods .	1,450
24	,, Selling Expenses .	10			
31	,, Share of Profit (to Profit and Loss A/c) .	279			
31	, Bank—S. Green	661			
		£1,450			£1,450

From information supplied by Green and Grey is prepared the—

MEMORANDUM JOINT VENTURE ACCOUNT

Dr.   S. GREEN AND D. GREY   Cr.

		£			£
To Purchases . .		1,500	By Proceeds of Sale:		
,, Expenses . .		28	Grey . .		1,450
,, Selling Expenses:			Green . .		650
Green . .		4			
,, Selling Expenses:					
Grey . .		10			
,, Balance—being					
Profit . .	c/d	558			
		£2,100			£2,100
To Share of Profit—.			By Profit . .	b/d	558
S. Green (½) .		279			
D. Grey (½) .		279			
		£558			£558

It should be noted that the cheque for £500 sent by Grey to
Green does not appear in the Memorandum Account, neither
does the cheque in settlement for £661. This is because both
these cheques are simply transfers of money between the
"partners" and do not affect the profit in any way, whereas
the Memorandum Account is compiled for the purpose of
ascertaining the profit and will include only figures relevant to
that end.

EXERCISE 24

W. Jones and T. Bright join in the purchase of a cargo of wine with the
intention of sharing the profit equally. Jones paid the purchase price £2,500
and import duties and expenses £700. Bright was responsible for the sale of
the wine. He sold if for £4,100, and incurred distribution and other expenses
totalling £160.

Prepare the statement of profit and show the account in the books of each.

EXERCISE 25

M. Robson entered into a joint venture with B. Younger. Robson purchased
goods £1,200 and received Younger's cheque for half that sum. Robson
incurred expenses: transport £22 and insurance £12. Younger sold £900
worth of the goods for £1,300 and Robson sold £200 worth for £270 and it
was agreed he should take over the balance unsold at cost. Selling and distribution expenses were: Younger £30; Robson £6. Profits are to be shared:
Robson ⅖, Younger ⅗.

Prepare the Memorandum Account and the account in the books of each
party to the venture.

EXERCISE 26

S. Barton and C. Todd entered into a joint venture. Barton purchased goods £1,000 and paid expenses £20. Todd purchased goods £3,000 and paid expenses £46; then he sent the goods to Barton for sale and the latter sold all the goods for £4,500.

Prepare the Memorandum Account and the account as it would appear in the books of each. Profits are to be shared equally.

CHAPTER VII

SELF BALANCING LEDGERS

WITH the growth of a business the more numerous the transactions become and the more the work of recording the transactions increases. A point is reached when it is necessary to subdivide the work among a larger staff. To facilitate the division of labour several ledgers may be brought into use, instead of the two or three previously used. A simple division, as students will already be aware, is to separate the accounts of debtors and creditors, and have a Sales Ledger and a Bought Ledger. It is seldom that transactions in both directions occur, so that a case arising where purchases are made from a customer presents no difficulty. The division, of course, will be made to suit the particular needs of the firm. It may be considered more practicable to have the following—

Private Ledger containing the Capital and Drawings Accounts of the owners, and the Trading Account, Profit and Loss Account, and Balance Sheets from year to year.

Nominal or General Ledger, containing the Real and Nominal Accounts.

Bought Ledger, containing the Creditor's Accounts for purchases made, and the

Sales Ledger, containing the Debtors' Accounts for goods sold.

As transactions become more numerous still the Bought Ledger and Sales Ledger may be subdivided. Such subdivision may be on an alphabetical basis as, for example, one Bought Ledger may contain the accounts of creditors whose names begin with a letter from A to M. A second Bought

Ledger would be used for creditors from N to Z. Similarly, three Sales Ledgers might be necessary and would be used, respectively, for customers the initial letter of whose names came within A to K, L to R, and S to Z.

Another basis might be preferred as, for example, the geographical, as Town, Country, and Foreign.

Obviously, a Trial Balance extracted from any one of these Ledgers would be useless. The Bought Ledger, for example, contains the creditors' accounts only. The compensating double entry for each item is to be found in some other Ledger, e.g. the debit entry for cash paid is in the Bought Ledger, but the credit entry is in the Cash Book.

If, however, a special account was raised in the Bought Ledger in which all the items in the accounts in that Ledger were entered (in total) but on opposite sides, then for every credit would be found a debit within the Ledger and a Trial Balance for the Bought Ledger only could be extracted. Similarly for each Ledger.

Such a device of incorporating a special account within the Ledgers renders the Ledger "self-balancing."

The chief purpose is to localize errors by proving each book separately, and it is then known within which book a possible error has occurred. Without such sectional proof there is no means of knowing where an error shown by the overall Trial Balance is, and much time and trouble is involved in the effort to locate it.

Formerly, accounts for the checking of the Sales Ledger and Bought Ledger balances were raised only in the General Ledger. Then the idea was extended to the opening of similar accounts, but with sides reversed, in each of the Sales Ledgers and Bought Ledgers. This yielded the self- or sectional-balancing principle, and gave corresponding credit and debit entries for the entries in the checking accounts in the General Ledger. It should be remembered, however, that these accounts are memorandum accounts only, raised for the special purpose of providing an internal check on the accuracy of the books, and are not part of the financial record proper.

Adjustment Accounts

The special accounts raised are known as Adjustment Accounts. An Adjustment Account is constructed for the Bought Ledger (separate accounts for each subdivision, if any), and appears in the General Ledger as the Bought Ledger Adjustment or Control Account. A corresponding account with the sides reversed, so that the double entry exists between the two accounts, appears in the Bought Ledger, and is headed "General Ledger Adjustment Account."

Similarly, a Sales Ledger Adjustment or Control Account for each Sales Ledger appears in the General Ledger, and a corresponding account, with the items on the opposite sides, is raised in the Sales Ledger under the heading "General Ledger Adjustment Account."

If it is borne in mind that the Adjustment Account (in the Sales Ledger, for example) contains in briefer form the information already in the Debtors' Accounts, its construction is simplified.

The entries in the Debtors' Accounts in the Sales Ledger may be classified as follows—

Debits

1. The opening balances of the accounts as at the beginning of the period.

2. Entries for goods sold during the period.

3. Dishonoured cheques and bills receivable dishonoured.

Credits

1. Cash received from debtors.

2. Allowances and discounts allowed.

3. Returns inwards.

4. Bills receivable.

5. Other credits (if any) not included under 1–4 above (e.g. bad debts and contra entries).

The Adjustment Account in the Sales Ledger would therefore contain this information, but on opposite sides to those in the Debtors' Accounts. Such an account may be drawn up as on the opposite page.

GENERAL LEDGER ADJUSTMENT ACCOUNT

Dr.   (IN THE SALES LEDGER)   Cr.

Jan. 31	To Total Cash received . .		£ 50,000	Jan. 1	By Total Debtors' balances at start . .	b/d	£ 10,000
	„ Total Discounts allowed . .		1,000	31	„ Total Sales for the month .		80,000
	„ Total Returns Inwards .		500				
	Total Bills Receivable .		8,500				
	„ Total Debtors' balances at close of the month .	c/d	30,000				
			£90,000				£90,000

In the General Ledger would appear the contra Adjustment Account as below—

SALES LEDGER ADJUSTMENT (OR CONTROL) ACCOUNT

Dr.   (IN THE GENERAL LEDGER)   Cr.

Jan. 1	To Total Debtors' balances at start . .	b/d	£ 10,000	Jan. 31	By Total Cash received . .		£ 50,000
31	„ Total Sales for the month .		80,000		„ Total Discounts allowed .		1,000
					„ Total Returns Inwards . .		500
					Total Bills Receivable .		8,500
					„ Total Debtors' balances at close of the month .	c/d	30,000
			£90,000				£90,000

The requisite entries for the Adjustment Accounts are obtained as follows—

1. The total debtors' balances at commencement of the period will be obtainable from the Trial Balance at the close of the previous period. The entry is made direct to the credit of the General Ledger Adjustment Account in the Sales Ledger, and the contra entry to the Sales Ledger Adjustment Account in the General Ledger.

2. Periodically (usually every month) the totals from the subsidiary books are posted to the Adjustment Accounts (these are, of course, additional to the normal postings from Sales Journal to personal accounts and Sales Accounts, etc.), so that the total sales for the month are posted from the Sales Journal to the credit of the General Ledger Adjustment Account in the Sales Ledger and to the debit of the Sales Ledger Adjustment Account in the General Ledger.

The debit entries of the General Ledger Adjustment Account in the Sales Ledger, which will be credited to the Sales Ledger Adjustment Account in the General Ledger, will be obtained from the following sources—

From the Cash Book. Total Cash received from Debtors during the period. Total Discounts allowed.

From Bills Receivable Book. Total Bills Receivable.

From Returns Inwards Journal. Total Returns and Allowances.

From the Journal. Allowances and other items not entered in any other subsidiary book.

On completion of the entries the balance of the Adjustment Account in the Sales Ledger should equal the total of the balances in the Debtors' Accounts. If such agreement is made, then the accuracy of the Sales Ledger may be assumed and the Adjustment Account has served its main purpose as a method of proof.

Adjustment Accounts for the Bought Ledger are similarly prepared. The total balances due to creditors at the start of the period is known, and the Purchases Journal provides the information of the total purchases for the period. The other items will come from the Cash Book, Bills Payable Book, and Returns Outwards Journal. The following is a specimen of an Adjustment Account as it would appear in the General Ledger—

BOUGHT LEDGER ADJUSTMENT (OR CONTROL) ACCOUNT

Dr. (IN THE GENERAL LEDGER) Cr.

			£					£
Jan. 31	To Total Cash Paid		25,000	Jan. 1	By Total Creditors at this date	b/d	8,000	
	,, Total Discount received		500	31	,, Total Purchases for the month		30,000	
	,, Total Bills Payable		1,500					
	,, Total Returns and allow-ances		1,000					
	,, Balance (Total Creditors' balances at close)	c/d	10,000					
			£38,000				£38,000	

The General Ledger Adjustment Account in the Bought Ledger would contain similar items but with the sides reversed, the account being posted from the same sources as the Adjustment Account in the General Ledger.

Special Items

Care must be exercised that all the items appearing in the personal accounts are contained in the Adjustment Accounts. There may be transfers from one Ledger to another on a change of name or the taking over of an account by a new firm. Interest on overdue accounts or on renewed bills may have been entered in the appropriate accounts, and should be debited or credited to the Adjustment Accounts.

The above examples have been based on the assumption that one Bought Ledger, one Sales Ledger, and a General Ledger existed. If the Ledgers are subdivided further, the information required for the Adjustment Accounts in each of the Ledgers will be more difficult to obtain unless the subsidiary books are ruled specially with this end in view. Separate Purchases Journals and Sales Journals may be kept to coincide in division with the subdivisions of the Ledgers, or the Purchases and Sales Journals may contain suitable analysis columns. For example, if two Bought Ledgers, A—M, N—Z, are kept, two separate Purchases Journals, A—M and N—Z,

CASH BOOK
(RECEIPTS SIDE ONLY)

Dr.

Date	Particulars	Folio	Discount	Cash	Bank	Sales Ledgers		
						A–K	L–R	S–Z
19.. Jan. 1	To A. Smith .	10	£	£	£ 20	£	£	£ 20

may be in use or, alternatively, a Purchases Journal with additional cash columns for analysis purposes, e.g.,

PURCHASES JOURNAL

Date	Particulars	Folio	Total	Ledgers	
				A–M	N–Z
			£	£	£

A similar analysis would be made in the Sales Journal, the Returns Journals, and the Bills Books. The Journal Proper, also, should contain extra columns for the Bought Ledger and Sales Ledger to provide for suitable analysis of the special items not passed through the usual subsidiary books.

The Cash Book, too, should contain additional cash columns for the analysis of the total columns. If two Bought Ledgers and three Sales Ledgers are in use there should be two additional columns on the credit side, and three additional columns on the debit side. The debit side is shown on page 46.

In the absence of analysed subsidiary books it is necessary to make the analysis periodically, and to assist in this lengthy task it is sometimes arranged that the clerk posting the items should add a distinguishing mark in the folio column to indicate to which Ledger the item has been posted.

EXERCISE 27

At 1st December, 19.., the Sales Ledger Control Account in the Private Ledger of Mason & Stone (who keep their Ledger on the self-balancing principle) showed a debit balance of £7,029. During the following month the sales amounted to £64,209. Returns inwards being £984. The amount of Cash Received during this month and posted to the Sales Ledger was £55,097, and Discounts allowed on accounts in this Ledger amounted to £2,118. There were transfers from the Bought Ledger to the credit of the Sales Ledger amounting to £895 and transfers from the Sales Ledger to the debit of the Bought Ledger totalling £1,759. Bills Receivable posted to the Sales Ledger amounted to £3,520, and there was a total of £219 transferred from this Ledger to the Bad Debts Account. From these particulars write up the Sales Ledger Control Account and bring down the balance at 31st December and state what this balance represents.

(U.L.C.I.)

EXERCISE 28

What is the object of making a Ledger Adjustment Account? Set out the following items as they would appear in an account of this kind in the Sales Ledger on 31st January, 19..—

	£
Credit Sales	35,000
Discount allowed to debtors	2,000
Cash received from debtors	21,000
Bills accepted by debtors	5,000
Bills dishonoured by debtors	500
Bad debts written off	1,000
Credit sales returns	1,500
Sundry debtors, 1st Jan.	10,000

(*N.C.T.E.C.*)

EXERCISE 29

From the following items prepare a Total Debtors Account, and show the amount outstanding at 31st December, 19..

		£
Jan. 1.	Total Debtors at this date	14,883
Dec. 31.	Cash received from customers during the year . .	132,532
	Goods sold to customers during the year . .	175,376
	Discount allowed to customers during the year . .	3,498
	Goods returned by customers during the year . .	3,767
	Acceptances received from customers . .	10,398
	Acceptances dishonoured	751
	Bad Debts written off	1,753

(*R.S.A.*)

EXERCISE 30

The following Total Account was prepared for a Sales Ledger for the purpose of self-balancing.

Dr.   SALES LEDGER TOTAL ACCOUNT   *Cr.*

	£		£
To Debtors, 1st Jan. . .	1,768	By Cash	3,213
,, Sales . . .	3,409	,, Discount . . .	83
,, Transfers . .	78	,, Returns . . .	108
,, Creditors, 31st Dec. .	27	,, Bills Receivable . .	62
		,, Debtors, 31st Dec. .	1,793
	£5,282		£5,259
To Debtors, 31st Dec. .	1,793		

Explain in detail what steps should be taken to rectify this account.

(*U.E.I.*)

EXERCISE 31

The following is an extract from the "Adjustment Account" in one of the Sales Ledgers of a business which balances all its Ledgers monthly—

			£				£
Feb. 28	To Cash .		4,518·77	Feb. 1	By Balance .	b/d	9,172·15
	,, Discount .		209·86	28	,, Sales . .		4,321·25
			57·50		,, Carriage .		43·06
	,, Balance .	c/d	8,762·83		,, Transfer K–P Sales		
					Ledger .		12·50
			£13,548·96				£13,548·96
				Mar. 1	By Balance .	b/d	8,762·83

Explain the meaning of each of the items appearing in this account and state from which books the several entries are posted.

(R.S.A.)

CHAPTER VIII

PARTNERSHIP ACCOUNTS

A PARTNERSHIP subsists where two or more persons carry on a business together with a view of making a profit. Because of the joint ownership by two or more persons of a business it is necessary to have records of the financial relationship of each to the partnership firm. The trading accounts are not affected. The records of purchases and sales, and other ordinary transactions of a trading concern, are similar under any form of ownership, whether that of a sole trader, a partnership firm, or limited company.

The accounts that are necessary in all partnerships have been considered in *Book-keeping, Stage I,* and it is assumed that the reader has studied that preliminary part of the subject. The following will suffice as a reminder of the essential points—

1. Partnerships are governed by the Partnership Act, 1890.

2. The partners are jointly (and in Scotland jointly and separately) liable for the debts of the firm.

3. Limited partners are allowed under the Limited Partnership Act, 1907. Such persons contribute capital to the business, but must take no active part. Liability of such persons for debts of the firm is limited to the capital sum contributed.

4. The following accounts are opened, in addition to the ordinary records of business transactions—

(*a*) Separate Capital Accounts for each partner.

(*b*) Separate Drawings (or Current) Accounts for each partner, to which is credited all that is due to the partner (share of profits, interest on capital, etc.) from the firm, and to which is debited all that the partner draws out or is liable for to the firm.

Other accounts are required should the partnership agreement provide for—

(a) Interest on capital.

(b) Interest on drawings.

(c) Payment of a salary to a partner.

The usual practice is for the Capital Account to remain untouched until such time that the capital sums are altered by withdrawal or addition. The Capital and Current Accounts are usually shown separately in detail in the Balance Sheet. Further, the net trading profit of the firm is carried down to a second section of the Profit and Loss Account. This section, called the Appropriation Account, then contains a record of the trading profit and its allocation among the partners.

The reader is advised to refresh his memory on these points by referring to the appropriate chapters in *Book-keeping, Stage I.*

EXERCISE 32

Explain why, where persons are trading in partnership, it is customary to credit each partner with interest on his capital before the balance of profit is ascertained and divided.

If there is any particular case where you consider such a provision might equitably be dispensed with, describe it and state shortly your reason for making this exception to the general rule.

(*R.S.A.*)

EXERCISE 33

Black and White are in partnership. No partnership deed has been prepared, and no agreement entered into with regard to the sharing of profits or interest on capital. Any loans were to be allowed 4 per cent interest. Black contributed £4,000 capital, and a loan of £1,000, and White contributed £1,000 capital. Prior to charging any interest, the profits of the partnership for the year amounted to £960. Show by means of an account the division of profits between the partners.

(*N.C.T.E.C.*)

EXERCISE 34

The Partnership Agreement between A, B, and C contains the following provisions—

   (a) The partners' *fixed* Capitals shall be—A, £10,000; B, £8,000; C, £6,000.
   (b) A and B are each to receive a salary of £600 a year.
   (c) Interest on capital is to be calculated at 5 per cent per annum.
   (d) A, B, and C are to share profits and losses in the ratio 3:2:1.
   (e) No interest is to be charged on Drawings or Current Accounts.
   On 1st January, 19..., the balances on Current Accounts were: A, Cr. £500; B, Cr. £200; C, Cr. £350.

During the year the drawings were: A, £1,200; B, £1,000; and C, £500. The Profit and Loss Account for the year showed a profit of £4,500 before charging interest on Capital and Partners' Salaries.
   Show the Capital and Current Accounts of A, B, and C, as at 31st December, after the division of the profit.

(U.E.I.)

EXERCISE 35

A. Potter and C. Fry are partners, who commence trading as wholesale butter merchants, sharing the profits and losses in the proportions of two-thirds and one-third respectively. A. Potter puts £4,000 and C. Fry £2,000 into the business, all of which is paid into the account opened at the Bank on 1st January, 19..
   Open the books of the firm at 1st January, 19.. and record the following transactions—

19..
Jan. 1. Cashed cheque for £100 for office purposes.
      2. Paid for warehouse and office premises by cheque, £3,750.
      3. Paid for office furniture and fittings, £162, by cheque.
      4. Purchased, on credit, 20 tons of butter at £7·60 per cwt. from Danish Butter Merchants Ltd.
      5. Purchased, on credit, 10 tons of butter at £7·50 per cwt. from Jorgansens & Co.
      6. Sold, on credit, 1 ton butter at £8·40 per cwt. to Lacey Bros.
      9. Paid, by cash, wages, £17·75.
    11. Sold, on credit, 15 tons of butter at £8·10 per cwt. to Farmers, Ltd.
    13. Received cheque from Farmers, Ltd., in settlement of their account, less 2½ per cent cash discount.
    16. Sold on credit, 10 tons of butter at £8 per cwt., to Shire & Co.
    18. Paid, by cash, wages, £17·75.
    19. Received cheque for £100 from Lacey Bros. on account.
    21. Paid Danish Butter Merchants Ltd., by cheque, the balance of their account, less 2½ per cent cash discount.
    23. Paid, by cheque, £52·50 for new typewriter.

Jan. 25. Paid, by cash, wages, £17·75.

28. Received cheque from Shire & Co. in settlement of their account.

31. Received cheque for £25 in respect of rent of part of the premises that have been let.

31. Notice received that Lacey Bros. have become insolvent, and there is no likelihood of receiving any of the amount due from them.

The stock at 31st January was valued at £440.

(a) Balance the Ledger Accounts and extract a Trial Balance.

(b) Close the Ledger Accounts and prepare Trading Account and Profit and Loss Account for the month of January, 19.., and a Balance Sheet at 31st January, 19...

(R.S.A.)

EXERCISE 36

From the Trial Balance and other information given below you are required to prepare a Trading Account, Profit and Loss Account, and a Balance Sheet as at 31st March, 19...

W. FREEMAN & SON

TRIAL BALANCE, 31st March, 19..

	£	£
Capital Account, Wm. Freeman		2,000
,, ,, John Freeman		500
Drawings ,,	360	
Cash in hand	29	
Bank		128
Rent and Rates	286	
Carriage Outwards	351	
Creditors		1,637
General Office Expenses	400	
Bad Debts	20	
Machinery and Plant	1,200	
Stock, 1st April, 19.	2,310	
Sales		10,936
Purchases	8,412	
Debtors	940	
Repairs to Machinery	86	
Discount	259	146
Bills Receivable	866	
Returns	138	310
	£15,657	£15,657

The following adjustments are to be made—

Depreciate machinery and plant at the rate of 5 per cent.

A debt of £170 included in sundry debtors is estimated to be worth only 10s. in the £.

Interest to be allowed on capital at 5 per cent per annum.

W. Freeman takes two-fifths and John Freeman three-fifths of the net profit.

Stock on hand 31st March, 19.. was valued at £1,700.

(U.L.C.I.)

EXERCISE 37

The following balances were extracted from the books of Messrs. Brown and Thomas on the 31st March, 19.. after a full year's trading—

Dr.	£	Cr.	£
Land and Buildings	4,960	Creditors	1,327
Plant and Machinery	3,000	Provision for Bad Debts	66
Stock in hand, 1st April	2,019	Sales	14,274
Debtors	1,600	Returns Outwards	870
Purchases	9,284	Discount	29
General Expenses	150	A. Brown, Capital	5,000
Returns Inwards	370	B. Thomas, ,,	3,000
Manufacturing Wages	2,001	Provision for Depreciation of	
Rates and Taxes	167	Plant and Machinery	2,000
Insurance	66		
Manufacturing Expenses	225		
Salaries	666		
Discount	36		
Cash in hand	64		
Cash at Bank	658		
Drawings—			
A. Brown	1,000		
B. Thomas	300		
	£26,566		£26,566

From the above particulars you are required to prepare Trading and Profit and Loss Accounts, and a Balance Sheet, after taking into account the following adjustments: Depreciation on Land and Buildings, 2½ per cent; on Plant and Machinery, 10 per cent. The provision for bad debts is to be increased to 5 per cent on the sundry debtors. Unexpired amounts to be carried forward: Rates, £27; Insurance, £16. The partnership agreement provides: (a) that 5 per cent shall be allowed on partnership capital (no interest on drawings), (b) that the net profit shall be divided between the partners *pro rata* to the amounts to the credit of their capital accounts at the commencement of the period. Stock in hand on 31st March, 19.., £1,990.

(N.C.T.E.C.)

EXERCISE 38

The following balances were extracted from the books of Messrs. Milner and Mercer on 31st December, 19.., after a full year's trading—

Dr.	£	Cr.	£
Land and Buildings	6,300	Loan from H. Wilson at 5%	4,000
Machinery and Plant	9,000	Sales	20,465
Office Furniture	780	Rent from Garage	41
J. Milner, Current Account	378	Provision for Doubtful Debts	138
W. Mercer, ,, ,,	141	Discount	387
Purchases	14,187	Sundry Creditors	1,515
Wages	4,544	Bank	328
Office Salaries	189	Bills Payable	338
Travellers' Salaries	432	Capital—	
Rates and Insurance	121	J. Milner	8,600
Discount	1,064	W. Mercer	5,600
Repairs	248	Provision for Depreciation	
Gas and Water	184	of Furniture	650
Commissions	123	Provision for Depreciation of	
Travelling Expenses	269	Machinery	2,750
Bank Charges	68		
Returns Inward	143		
Trade Expenses	179		
Stock in hand, 1st Jan.	3,611		
Sundry Debtors	2,706		
Cash in hand	5		
Interest	140		
	£44,812		£44,812

From the above particulars you are required to prepare Trading and Profit and Loss Accounts, and a Balance Sheet, after taking into account the following adjustments, etc.: The partners share profits and losses equally after being credited with interest on their respective capital accounts at the rate of 5 per cent. No interest on current accounts. Depreciate the machinery and plant at the rate of 5 per cent. The provision for doubtful debts must be made equal to 5 per cent of the sundry debtors. The stock in hand was valued at £7,050.

(N.C.T.E.C.)

EXERCISE 39

A. Johnson, B. Campbell, and C. Orr are partners trading as Importers and Agents under the style of "Johnson & Co." They share profits in the ratio $\frac{1}{2}$, $\frac{1}{3}$, $\frac{1}{6}$.

The following list of balances, extracted from their books as at 31st December 19.., is complete, with the exception that the balance of Bank Account has been left out—

							£
Capital: A. Johnson	.	.	.	.	.	.	2,777
,, B. Campbell	.	.	.	.	.	.	3,020

	£
Capital: C. Orr	1,482
Drawings: A. Johnson	1,200
„ B. Campbell	840
„ C. Orr	720
Cash in hand	17
Purchases	11,860
Sales	16,923
Stock, 1st January	4,530
Allowance Received on Purchases	171
Sales Returns and Allowances	92
Carriage	311
Rent and Rates	377
Salaries and Travellers' Commissions	1,642
Customs Duty	926
Commission Earned	2,482
Sundry Expenses	139
Freight and Marine Insurance	332
Bank Charges and Interest	36
Bad Debts	140
Bad Debts Provision, 1st January	223
Discounts Allowed	362
Discounts Received	288
Stationery and Advertising	95
Bills Payable	791
Depreciation	83
Sundry Debtors	7,073
Bills Receivable	27
Interest Receivable	14
Sundry Creditors	2,838
Motor Vans	255
Furniture and Fittings	152

You are required to prepare a Trial Balance, Trading and Profit and Loss
Accounts, and Balance Sheet, noting that—

(a) The item Carriage includes £95 for Carriage Inwards.

(b) The stock as at 31st December, is valued as follows: Cost Price, £5,021;
Market Value, £4,705.

(c) There are outstanding expenses as follows: Freight, £47; Travellers'
Commissions, £28.

(d) There is a considerable quantity of unused Stationery, valued by the
partners at £31.

(e) The new Bad Debts Provision is to be 3 per cent of the Sundry Debtors,
including Bills Receivable.

(f) The item "Depreciation" is made up as follows: Furniture and Fittings,
5 per cent on £160; Motor Vans, 25 per cent on £300.

Journal entries are not required, but great attention should be paid to the
order in which the items are arranged in the Trading and Profit and Loss
Accounts and Balance Sheet.

(U.E.I.)

EXERCISE 40

On 31st December, 19.., a fire occurred in the offices of Alpha, Beta, & Co., and the books of the company were destroyed. The following list of balances taken out at the close of business on that date was, however, preserved—

	£
A. Alpha—Capital	1,405·72
B. Beta—Capital	702·86
Lease of premises	1,800·00
Bank—Deposit Account—Balance in hand	1,000·00
Current Account ,, ,, ,,	390·81
Cash in hand	27·26
Sales	11,576·59
Sales Returns	176·35
Purchases	7,776·35
Purchases Returns	29·52
Rent Received	104·00
Discount allowed	115·13
Rates and Water	80·33
Telephone	20·11
Lighting and Heating	50·55
Stock	1,001·15
Discount Received	35·33
Insurance	15·42
Debtors	1,059·56
Plant and Machinery	510·00
Repairs and Renewals	31·04
Wages—office	577·00
A. Alpha—Drawings	250·00
B. Beta—Drawings	250·00
Creditors	397·54
Fixtures and Fittings	120·50
A. Alpha—Loan to firm	1,000·00

1. You are required to prepare Trading and Profit and Loss Accounts for the year ending 31st December, 19.., and Balance Sheet at that date.

2. Open a new set of books for the firm at the commencement of business on 1st January, 19...

The firm of Alpha, Beta & Co. is carried on by two partners, A. Alpha and B. Beta, and they share the profits and losses of the business in the proportions of two-thirds and one-third respectively.

In preparing the accounts, the following matters must be taken into consideration—

(a) Stock on hand at 31st December, 19.., was valued at £1576·32.

(b) The lease of the premises for a period of 10 years was purchased on 1st January, two years ago, for £2,000, to be written off in equal annual instalments over the 10 years.

(c) Depreciation at the rate of 7½ per cent per annum on cost, £551 to be written off Plant and Machinery.

(d) A provision of £50 to be made in respect of a doubtful debt.

(e) A provision for a full year's interest at the rate of 6 per cent per annum to be made on the loan of A. Alpha. (R.S.A.)

CHAPTER IX

PARTNERSHIP ACCOUNTS:
ADMISSION OF PARTNER AND GOODWILL

A SOLE trader or an existing partnership firm may find it necessary or desirable to bring in a new partner. The occasion may arise from the need for more capital, or to have additional help in the supervision of the business. The newcomer, however, enters into an existing business, the present, and much of the future, profits of which are derived from the efforts of the old partners or owner. Goodwill has been created though it is not recorded, and the new partner becomes entitled to a share in it. The question arises whether the new partner should or should not make some payment, additional to the capital he brings with him, for this opportunity.

If the new partner makes such payment it is called a PREMIUM for his admission to partnership, and is, of course, separate from the capital introduced.

Example

A and B trading in partnership each with a capital of £5,000, sharing profits equally, admit C as partner on his introducing £3,000 as capital and paying £2,000 as premium for his admission to the firm.

In the new firm profits to be shared A $\frac{2}{5}$, B $\frac{2}{5}$, C $\frac{1}{5}$.

The sum of £3,000 will be paid into the firm's banking account and debited in the Cash Book. C's Capital Account will be credited with the like sum.

The premium may be dealt with in one of the following ways—

Example No. 1

If so agreed the premium is paid *direct* to A and B in the proportion in which they shared profits, no entries being made in the books.

Example No. 2

The premium is paid to A and B, but the transaction is passed through the firm's books *as a record only*.

METHOD

Debit Cash £2,000.
Credit A's Current (or Drawings) Account with £1,000.
Credit B's Current (or Drawings) Account with £1,000.
Credit Cash on the amounts being paid to A and B.
Debit £1,000 to A's Current Account.
Debit £1,000 to B's Current Account.

Dr.			CASH BOOK		Cr.
	£				£
To C's Capital .	3,000		By A (being withdrawal of premium) .		1,000
„ C's Premium .	2,000		„ B (being withdrawal of premium) .		1,000

Dr.		A's CAPITAL		Cr.
	£			£
		By Balance .	b/d	5,000

Dr.		B's CAPITAL		Cr.
	£			£
		By Balance .	b/d	5,000

Dr.		C's CAPITAL		Cr.
	£			£
		By Cash .	CB	3,000

Dr.	A's Current Account					Cr.
	To Cash (with-drawal of premium)	£ 1,000		By Cash (¼ C's premium) .		£ 1,000

Dr.	B's Current Account					Cr.
	To Cash (with-drawal of premium)	£ 1,000		By Cash (¼ C's premium) . .		£ 1,000

Example No. 3

A, B, C agree that the premium is to be paid into the firm and left in the business.

As the premium is by way of compensation to A and B for what they forgo when C joins them, it is their property, but, in this case, is used for the benefit of the new partnership firm.

METHOD

Debit Cash Account with the £2,000 paid in.

Credit A's Capital Account with half share, £1,000.

Credit B's Capital Account with half share, £1,000.

(The premium is divided in the proportion in which the old partners shared profits.)

The transaction may be regarded as, in effect, similar to Example No. 1 above, the premium being paid direct to A and B, but that A and B go a step further and pay the sums received into the firm as additional capital.

Dr.	CASH BOOK					Cr.
	To C's Capital . „ C's Premium .	£ 3,000 2,000				£

Dr.	A's Capital					Cr.
		£		By Balance . „ Cash—½ share of C's premium .	b/d	£ 5,000 1,000

Dr.			B's Capital			*Cr.*
	£		By Balance . .	b/d		£ 5,000
			,, Cash—½ share of C's premium .			1,000

Dr.			C's Capital			*Cr.*
	£		By Cash .			£ 3,000

It is important to note that in the above three examples the old partners have been compensated in cash for the share in the goodwill they forgo by the admission of C as a new partner, and therefore there has been no occasion to open a "Goodwill Account" in the books of the firm.

Raising a Goodwill Account

The new partner C may have no cash resources beyond the £3,000 which it is agreed he shall introduce as capital. He is therefore not in a position to pay a premium to A and B, and some other way must be found to compensate the old partners.

Example

A and B trading as equal partners, each with a capital of £5,000, admit C as partner on his introducing £3,000 as capital. C pays no premium but it is agreed that a goodwill account of £2,000 shall be raised and that A and B shall be credited with a similar amount in the proportion in which they shared profits.

On the admission of a new partner, a new partnership firm is created. The assets of the new firm comprise the assets of the old firm plus a new asset, Goodwill, valued at £2,000. The goodwill was created by the old firm, A and B, and instead of being paid in cash, A and B become the creditors of the new firm, A, B, and C, for the amount.

Method

Open Goodwill Account and debit to it the sum of £2,000.
Credit A's Capital Account, £1,000.

Credit B's Capital Account, £1,000.

The Goodwill will appear in the Balance Sheet of the new firm as an asset offset by the increased liability of the firm to A and B.

JOURNAL

			£	£
Goodwill Account *Dr.*	L1	2,000		
To A's Capital	L2			1,000
,, B's ,, ...	L3			1,000
Being goodwill raised in the books and credited to A's and B's Capital Accounts on entry of C as partner. (Per partnership agreement dated . . .)				

Dr.			GOODWILL (1)				*Cr.*
			£				£
To Sundries .	J		2,000				

Dr.			A's CAPITAL (2)				*Cr.*
			£				£
				By Balance .	b/d		5,000
				Goodwill .	J		1,000

Dr.			B's CAPITAL (3)				*Cr.*
			£				£
				By Balance .	b/d		5,000
				,, Goodwill .	J		1,000

The £3,000 paid in by C as capital will be debited to Cash Account, and the same amount credited to C's Capital Account.

EXERCISE 41

A. Brown and P. Smith trading in equal partnership, each with a capital of £5,000, admit A. Jones as partner on his introducing £2,500 as capital and paying £1,000 as premium for his admission to the firm.

The new firm share profits as follows: Brown, $\frac{2}{5}$, Smith, $\frac{2}{5}$, Jones, $\frac{1}{5}$.

The premium is paid direct to Brown and Smith.

Show how the admission of the new partner affects the partnership accounts.

EXERCISE 42

Dunbar and Horne are in partnership and share profits and losses in proportion to their capitals which are, respectively, £5,000 and £3,000. They admit Reed as partner on his bringing into the business £3,000, which sum was duly paid into the firm's banking account. Of this sum, £2,000 represents Reed's capital and £1,000 his premium for admission to the partnership. The premium is paid out to the partners.

Record Reed's admission and the payment out of the premium in the partnership books.

EXERCISE 43

Small and Tall, trading in partnership and sharing profits equally, have each a capital of £4,000. Short is admitted as partner on condition that he brings into the new firm the sum of £3,000. Of this amount £2,000 is Short's capital and £1,000 is the premium for his admission to the firm. The premium is to remain in the business.

Give the entries to record his admission.

EXERCISE 44

Define the term "Goodwill."

A B takes C D into partnership, and it is agreed that the goodwill of A B's business is to be valued at £2,000. Give the entries necessary to record the goodwill in the books of the new firm.

(R.S.A.)

EXERCISE 45

Long and Wyde are in partnership under the firm name of Long and Company. Long's capital is £4,000 and Wyde's capital is £2,000, and profits are shared in proportion to capital held.

It is agreed to admit Wise as partner, but he has no other resources apart from £2,000 he is to introduce as capital. It is, therefore, arranged that a goodwill account for £1,500 shall be raised and the capital accounts of the original partners shall be credited in the proportion in which they shared profits.

Give the entries rendered necessary by Wise's admission on these terms.

EXERCISE 46

Young and Davis are partners with capital respectively of £8,000 and £4,000, and share profits in the same proportions as their capitals.

They arrange to admit Griffiths into partnership on condition that he pays in £2,000 as capital and £2,000 as premium. Griffiths cannot raise more than £3,000 so that the original agreement is modified. He is to pay in £2,000 as capital, £1,000 direct to Young and Davis as premium, and a Goodwill Account of £7,000 is to be raised.

Give the entries necessary to record the admission of Griffiths under the modified agreement.

CHAPTER X

PARTNERSHIP ACCOUNTS:
ACQUISITION OF A BUSINESS, DISSOLUTION OF PARTNERSHIPS, AMALGAMATION OF BUSINESSES, AND FINAL ADJUSTMENTS

AN opportunity may occur for the acquisition of a business as a going concern. Whether the purchase is made by a sole trader, partnership firm, or company, the taking over of the business with its current liabilities and assets will be recorded in similar manner, except in so far as the Partners' Capital Accounts or the company's Share Capital Account may be involved.

The valuation of the business is agreed on the basis of the Balance Sheet as on the particular day. The purchase price is mutually arranged and it may be in excess of the capital value of the business, such excess representing payment for goodwill. The assets only (with or without the cash in hand) or both assets and liabilities may be taken over.

The first steps to record the purchase require new accounts to be opened and the following entries to be made, viz.—

(a) *Debit* Purchase of Business Account.
   Credit Vendor's Account with the agreed purchase price.
   (NOTE. The vendor is the person selling the business.)
(b) Open an account for each asset required.
   Debit each asset, including goodwill (if any).
   Credit total of assets to Purchase of Business Account.
(c) *Debit* total of liabilities taken over to Purchase of Business Account.
   Open accounts for the liabilities taken over.
   Credit each liability to its account.
(d) *Debit* Vendor's Account.

Credit Cash Book with the payment of purchase price to Vendor.

When these steps have been taken the books should contain a completed record of the business as taken over. It will be seen that the Purchase of Business Account is but a temporary account to simplify the procedure of the transfer of the book entries.

Example

George Wright and Henry Dobson enter into partnership upon equal terms, to acquire the business carried on by Amos Atkinson. The business was taken over as at 1st January, 19.., on the basis of the last certified Balance Sheet, which was as follows—

BALANCE SHEET OF AMOS ATKINSON

AS AT 31ST DECEMBER, 19..

	£	£		£	£
Capital—			*Fixed Assets—*		
Amos Atkinson . .		26,000	Freehold Premises .	14,200	
			Plant and Machinery .	8,100	
Current Liabilities . .			Furniture and Fittings	600	
Sundry Creditors .	3,400				22,900
Provision for Bad			*Current Assets—* .		
Debts . . .	300		Stock-in-trade . .	4,100	
		3,700	Sundry Debtors .	2,700	
					6,800
		£29,700			£29,700

The purchase price was agreed at £28,000, and was paid in equal shares by Wright and Dobson direct to Atkinson. A Bank Account was opened in the name of the firm, into which each partner paid the sum of £1,000. For the purpose of the partnership the assets were revalued and the following reductions in value were made—

Plant and Machinery, £500; Stock, £450; and Furniture and Fittings, £200.

A Goodwill Account is to be raised in the partnership books for the difference between the total purchase price paid and the amended valuation.

You are required to make the Journal entries necessary to record the above transactions in the books of Messrs. Wright and Dobson, and prepare Balance Sheet as at the commencement of the new partnership.

(R.S.A.)

IN MESSRS. WRIGHT & DOBSON'S BOOKS
JOURNAL

		£	£
Purchase of Business		28,000	
To Vendor (Amos Atkinson) . . .			28,000
Being agreed purchase price of business. .			
Freehold Premises . . . . *Dr.*		14,200	
Plant and Machinery . . .		8,100	
Furniture and Fittings		600	
Stock-in-trade		4,100	
Sundry Debtors		2,700	
Goodwill		2,000	
To purchase of Business . . .			31,700
Being sundry assets acquired.			
Purchase of Business . . *Dr.*		3,700	
To Sundry Creditors . . .			3,400
,, Provision for Bad Debts . . .			300
Being sundry liabilities taken over.			
Vendor (Amos Atkinson) . . *Dr.*		28,000	
To Wright's Capital . . .			14,000
,, Dobson's ,, ...			14,000
Being agreed purchase price paid direct by partners to vendor.			
Goodwill . . . . . *Dr.*		1,150	
To Plant and Machinery . . .			500
,, Stock			450
,, Furniture and Fittings . . .			200
Being appreciation of goodwill on revaluation of assets.			

BALANCE SHEET

AS AT 1ST JANUARY

	£	£		£	£
Capital—			*Fixed Assets—*		
G. Wright . . .	15,000		Goodwill . .	3,150	
H. Dobson . .	15,000		Freehold Premises .	14,200	
		30,000	Plant and Machinery .	7,600	
Current Liabilities—	.		Furniture and Fittings	400	
Sundry Creditors	.	3,400			25,350
			Current Assets—		
			Stock-in-trade . .	3,650	
			Sundry		
			Debtors £2,700		
			Less Provision 300		
				2,400	
			Cash at Bank . .	2,000	
					8,050
		£33,400			£33,400

Dissolution of Partnership

A partnership may be dissolved (*a*) by mutual agreement between the partners, or (*b*) on the termination of the special undertaking for which the partnership was formed, or (*c*) on the death, bankruptcy, or lunacy of a partner.

On dissolution the assets of the partnership are applied as follows—

First, to the payment of outside creditors.

Secondly, to the repayment of loans from the partners.

Thirdly, to the repayment of partners' capital.

Any surplus remaining after the satisfaction of these claims is distributed among the partners in the proportion in which they shared profits.

A Balance Sheet is prepared as at the date from which the dissolution is to take effect, and the following steps are taken—

1. Open a Realization of Assets Account.

2. Through the Journal close each Asset Account, except cash by transfer to the debit of the Realization Account.

3. *Debit* Cash.

   Credit Realization Account with the proceeds of sale of the assets.

4. *Credit* Cash.
   Debit the respective liability accounts with the liabilities
   and loans (if any) paid off.
5. *Credit* Cash.
   Debit Realization Account with the expenses of the
   dissolution.

The balance of the Realization Account at this stage will
represent either a profit or a loss.

6. If a profit on dissolution—
   Debit Realization Account.
   Credit the partners' respective Capital Accounts.

If a loss on dissolution—

   Credit Realization Account.
   Debit the partners' respective Capital Accounts.

The profit or loss, as the case may be, on realization is
shared in the proportions in which the partners shared profits.

The balances of the partners' Capital Accounts should now
together equal the balance of cash in hand, and repayment of
the partners' capital should close the Cash Book and the
Capital Accounts.

Example

A and B trading in partnership decide, as on 31st March, 19.., to dissolve
partnership and to liquidate their business.

Their Balance Sheet as on that date was as follows—

BALANCE SHEET

AS AT 31ST MARCH, 19..

	£		£
Capital—A	2,000	Cash	1,800
Capital—B . . .	1,500	Sundry Debtors . .	2,800
Sundry Creditors . . .	2,750	Other Assets . . .	850
		Goodwill . . .	800
	£6,250		£6,250

Profits and losses are shared equally.

The Debtors realized £2,700, other Assets £950, and the Goodwill of the
business was sold for £400. The expenses of liquidation amounted to £100.

Prepare the necessary accounts to show the result of the realization as it would appear in the books of the firm and the position of the two partners as regards the disposal of the balance of cash remaining after satisfying the firm's liabilities.

(R.S.A.)

JOURNAL

	£	£
Realization Account	4,450	
To Sundry Assets—		
Debtors		2,800
Other Assets		850
Goodwill		800
Being transfer of assets on dissolution of partnership.		
A's Capital	250	
B's Capital	250	
To Realization Account . . .		500
Being transfer of loss on realization of assets.		

Dr.   REALIZATION ACCOUNT   Cr.

		£				£
To Sundry Assets .		4,450	By Cash (proceeds			
,, Cash (Expenses			of sale of			
of Dissolution) .		100	Assets)			
			Debtors .			2,700
			Other assets .			950
			Goodwill .			400
			,, Balance .	c/d		500
		£4,550				£4,550
To Balance .	b/d	500	By A's Capital .			250
			,, B's Capital .			250
		£500				£500

Dr.   CASH BOOK   Cr.

		£				£
To Balance .	b/d	1,800	By Sundry Cred-			
,, Proceeds of			itors .			2,750
sale of assets		4,050	,, Dissolution			
			Expenses .			100
			,, Balance .	c/d		3,000
		£5,850				£5,850
To Balance .	b/d	3,000				

Dr.   A's CAPITAL   Cr.

			£					£
To Realization Account .	.		250		By Balance	.	b/d	2,000
„ Balance .	.	c/d	1,750					
			£2,000					£2,000
					By Balance	.	b/s	1,750

Dr.   B's CAPITAL   Cr.

			£					£
To Realization Account .	.		250		By Balance	.	b/d	1,500
„ Balance .	.	c/d	1,250					
			£1,500					£1,500
					By Balance	.	b/d	1,250

The Capital Accounts show £1,750 to the credit of A and £1,250 to the credit of B at the conclusion of the realization of the assets, and a balance of cash in hand of £3,000. The payment out of the balance to the credit of A and B will close the Cash Account.

In the above worked example the realization has resulted in a loss, but the capital to the credit of the partners is in each case sufficient to cover the loss.

Had the amount to the credit of either or both partners been insufficient to meet the loss on realization, the partner or partners would have to bring in further cash from their private resources in sufficient amount to meet the loss.

Had a profit resulted, the amount of profit would have appeared on the debit side of the Realization Account, and would have been credited in the appropriate proportions to the partners' respective Capital Accounts.

Amalgamation of Two Businesses

A partnership may originate in two sole traders agreeing to amalgamate their existing businesses. As each is a going concern there will be assets and liabilities in each case, and an amalgamation usually requires the merging of these. The two sole traders will be concerned to see that each other's Balance Sheet presents a true statement of the financial position of the business, that assets are stated at their proper value, and that all liabilities are disclosed. A further consideration is the goodwill attaching to each concern. The matter is simplified if the businesses are of more or less equal importance. If there is inequality in value of the goodwill, then due allowance must be made to the owner of the more important concern in the formation of the new partnership firm.

Amalgamation being decided upon, each sole trader prepares his Balance Sheet as at that date. These are considered with a view of adjustments in the values shown being made as may be agreed upon. The Balance Sheets are drawn up afresh in the light of these adjustments and are combined to form the Balance Sheet of the new partnership firm.

If one party to the new partnership wishes to retain any of his own assets for himself, or if the other party objects to the inclusion of an asset, then, subject to the agreement by both parties, of course, this will have the effect of reducing the amount of capital brought in by the party concerned.

Example

S. Holmes and F. Brown agree to amalgamate their businesses as from 1st January, 19... Their respective balance sheets are as below—

S. HOLMES'S BALANCE SHEET

	£		£
Capital	6,900	Plant and Machinery	4,000
Sundry Creditors	600	Stock	1,500
		Furniture and Fittings	200
		Sundry Debtors	1,000
		Cash	800
	£7,500		£7,500

F. BROWN'S BALANCE SHEET

	£		£
Capital	1,600	Plant and Machinery .	1,000
Creditors	400	Stock	700
Overdraft	300	Furniture . . .	100
		Sundry Debtors .	500
	£2,300		£2,300

The opening Balance Sheet of the new partnership firm is to be prepared, taking into consideration the following adjustments: Holmes is to be credited with £2,000 for Goodwill. Brown's Machinery and Plant is to be reduced in value by 10 per cent. Both stocks are to be reduced 10 per cent. Brown is to pay off his overdraft from private means. A provision for bad debts at 5 per cent is to be made in both cases.

The first step is the redrafting of the Balance Sheets—

IN S. HOLMES'S BOOKS
JOURNAL

		£	£
Jan. 1	Capital . . . . . Dr.	200	
	To Stock		150
	,, Provision for Bad Debts . .		50
	Being reduction on revaluation.		
	Goodwill . . . . . Dr.	2,000	
	To Capital		2,000
	Being value of goodwill on amalgamation		

REDRAFTED BALANCE SHEET—S. HOLMES

	£	£		£
Capital . . .	6,900		Goodwill . . .	2,000
Add Goodwill . .	2,000		Plant and Machinery .	4,000
	8,900		Stock . .	1,350
Less loss on revaluation			Furniture and Fittings .	200
of Stock . .	150		Sundry Debtors	
	8,750		(*less* Provision) .	950
Less Provision for Bad			Cash . . .	800
Debts . . .	50	8,700		
Sundry Creditors .		600		
		£9,300		£9,300

IN F. BROWN'S BOOKS
JOURNAL

			£	£
Jan. 1	Capital . . . . . *Dr.*		195	
	To Plant and Machinery . . .			100
	„ Stock			70
	„ Provision for Bad Debts . .			25
	Being reduction on revaluation. .			

REDRAFTED BALANCE SHEET—F. BROWN

	£	£		£
Capital	1,600		Plant and Machinery .	900
Add Overdraft paid off .	300		Stock	630
			Furniture	100
	1,900		Sundry Debtors	
Less Loss on revaluation			(*less* Provision) . .	475
of Plant and Stock .	170			
	1,730			
Less Provision for Bad				
Debts . . .	25			
		1,705		
Sundry Creditors . .		400		
		———		———
		£2,105		£2,105

(*Note.* Brown's cancellation of the overdraft from private resources is in effect an increase of capital in the business.)

The next step is to combine the two new Balance Sheets into one Balance Sheet, showing the position of the partnership firm as at the date of its formation—

BALANCE SHEET OF HOLMES & BROWN—PARTNERS

	£	£		£	£
Capital—			*Fixed Assets—*		
S. Holmes . .	8,700		Goodwill . .	2,000	
F. Brown . .	1,705		Plant and Machinery .	4,900	
		10,405	Furniture and Fittings	300	
				———	7,200
Current Liabilities— .			*Current Assets—* .		
Sundry Creditors .		1,000	Sundry Debtors .	1,425	
			Stock . . .	1,980	
			Cash . . .	800	
				———	4,205
		———			———
		£11,405			£11,405

Adjustment of Final Accounts

In the preparation of the final accounts of a partnership from a given Trial Balance attention must be paid to all instructions regarding adjustments to be made. Apart from the general type of adjustment there may be special instructions arising from the form of ownership.

For example—

(a) The partnership deed provides that interest is to be allowed to partners at 5 per cent per annum on their Capital Accounts.

The entries in the Ledger would be to *debit* Interest on Capital Account with 5 per cent on the partners' Capitals as at the beginning of the trading period and *credit* the partners' respective Current Accounts. The balance of the Interest on Capital Account is transferred, on closing the books, to the debit of the appropriation section of the Profit and Loss Account.

Where final accounts only are being prepared the amount of interest is debited to the second (or appropriation) section of the Profit and Loss Account, and the appropriate amounts added to the balances of the partners' respective Current Accounts which appear in the Balance Sheet.

(b) Smith is to be allowed a partnership salary of £250 per annum.

This salary has not been paid as it would have then appeared in the given Trial Balance, and not as an accompanying instruction.

The sum of £250 should be credited to Smith's Current Account, and debited to Partnership Salary Account in the Ledger. In preparing final accounts from a given Trial Balance the £250 would be added to the balance of Smith's Current Account in the Balance Sheet, and debited to the appropriation section of the Profit and Loss Account.

(c) Goods (£100) were taken from stock by Smith, a partner, for his own use, but no entry had been made in the books.

This amounts to drawings on account of profit due to the partner in kind instead of cash.

Debit Smith's Current Account £100 and credit Purchases Account in the Ledger with a like sum.

In the final accounts from a given Trial Balance deduct £100 from the balance of Smith's Current Account in the Balance Sheet and credit Trading Account with a similar sum, or show as a deduction from Purchases.

Should it be a practice for the partners to take goods from stock, it is usual to open personal accounts in the Ledger under the partners' names to which the periodical withdrawals in kind are debited. At the close of the trading period such accounts are closed by the balances being transferred to the partners' respective Current Accounts.

EXERCISE 47

Kirk and Church decided to enter into partnership on equal terms to acquire as a going concern the business of R. Chapple. The basis of the transaction was the Balance Sheet dated 31st December, 19.., shown below and the business was taken over from the 1st January.

R. CHAPPLE'S BALANCE SHEET
AS AT 31ST DECEMBER, 19..

	£					£
Capital (R. Chapple) . .	8,000	Premises	.	.	.	3,000
Creditors	2,000	Fittings .	.	.	.	500
		Stock .	.	.	.	4,000
		Debtors .	.	.	.	1,800
		Cash .	.	.	.	700
	£10,000					£10,000

The purchase price was £9,800. Kirk and Church paid this sum in equal shares direct to Chapple. All the assets and liabilities were taken over except the cash (£700). Further Kirk and Church each paid £600 into the bank to open the new firm's banking account.

Show the entries in the partnership books to record the above transactions and draft the initial Balance Sheet of the firm.

EXERCISE 48

H. Wilson agrees to purchase the business of T. Trueman on the basis of the Balance Sheet given below for the sum of £5,500. Wilson is to take over all the liabilities and assets with the exception of the cash.

T. TRUEMAN'S BALANCE SHEET
AS AT 31ST MARCH, 19..

	£		£
Capital	4,800	Premises . . .	1,500
Creditors . . .	800	Furniture . . .	300
		Stock	2,000
		Debtors . . .	1,000
		Bills Receivable . .	200
		Cash . . .	600
	£5,600		£5,600

Make the necessary entries in Wilson's books on the assumption that he paid over the purchase price on 1st April, 19... Show also Wilson's opening Balance Sheet.

EXERCISE 49

Milne and Williams, trading in partnership and sharing profits three-fifths and two-fifths respectively, agree to dissolve partnership at 31st December, 19... The Balance Sheet at that date was as below—

BALANCE SHEET
AS AT 31ST DECEMBER, 19..

	£		£
Capital		Freehold Premises .	1,400
Milne	2,100	Furniture and Fittings .	300
Williams , . .	1,400	Stock . . .	1,600
Creditors	1,400	Debtors . . .	1,000
		Cash . . .	600
	£4,900		£4,900

The Premises, Furniture and Fittings, and Stock were disposed of for £4,000. The debtor's accounts were collected and realized £975. The creditors were paid in full and the realization expenses amounted to £100.

Prepare the necessary accounts to record the realization in the books of the firm.

EXERCISE 50

T. Jones and H. Fielding trading as equal partners decided to retire and dispose of the business as on 31st December, 19... The Balance Sheet at that date was as below—

BALANCE SHEET

	£		£
Capital		Freehold Premises . .	2,500
T. Jones . . .	5,000	Fixtures and Fittings .	700
H. Fielding . . .	5,000	Stock . . .	5,000
Sundry Creditors . .	2,200	Sundry Debtors . .	2,400
		Cash at Bank . .	1,600
	£12,200		£12,200

The Premises and Fixtures and Fittings realized £4,000. The Book Debts were collected and realized £2,100. The Stock was disposed of for £4,500. The Sundry Creditors were duly paid. The expenses of realization amounted to £100.

Prepare the accounts necessary to show the result of the realization.

EXERCISE 51

X and Y are equal partners, and on 31st January, 19.., their Balance Sheet is as follows—

	£		£
Capital—		Plant and Machinery .	550
X	1,200	Stock in hand . . .	1,300
Y	900	Sundry Debtors . .	700
Sundry Creditors . .	500	Cash in hand . .	50
	£2,600		£2,600

On this date they decided to dissolve the partnership and the assets realized as follows—

	£
Sundry Debtors	600
Stock	1,100
Plant and Machinery	300
Discount received from creditors . .	20
Expenses	80

Make the entries necessary to complete the above, and show the Ledger Accounts of the partners in their final form.

(*N.C.T.E.C.*)

EXERCISE 52

A. Adams and B. Bates were in partnership, sharing profits and losses two-thirds and one-third respectively. On 31st January, 19.., their Balance Sheet showed as follows—

	£		£
Sundry Creditors . .	1,800	Cash in hand . . .	70
Capital—		Sundry Debtors . .	3,600
A. Adams . . .	2,300	Stock in hand . . .	1,580
B. Bates . . .	1,150		
	£5,250		£5,250

On this date they decided to dissolve partnership and realize the assets. The stock realized £1,200 and the Sundry Debtors £3,150. The Sundry Creditors were paid and discount to the amount of £40 was received. The expenses of realization amounted to £18. Make the entries necessary to complete the above, and show the Ledger Accounts of the partners in their final form.

(N.C.T.E.C.)

EXERCISE 53

The following is a Balance Sheet of the firm A and B as on the 31st January, 19... The profits are shared as to A three-fourths and B one-fourth.

	£		£
Loan from W. James . .	200	Cash at Bank . . .	198
Sundry Creditors . .	660	Stock in hand . . .	430
Reserve Account . .	140	Sundry Debtors . .	550
Capital—A . . .	1,800	Furniture and Fixtures .	219
Capital—B . . .	600	Land and Buildings . .	2,003
	£3,400		£3,400

It was decided to dissolve the partnership and realize the assets, and the following arrangements were made: It was agreed that A should take over the land and buildings for £1,800, and B should take over the stock in hand at a discount of 10 per cent. The debtors realized £405, and the furniture and fixtures £169. The expenses of the realization amounted to £76. You are required to set out the accounts so as to show the results of the realization.

(N.C.T.E.C.)

EXERCISE 54

Dixon and Matthews, who are in partnership sharing profits two-thirds and one-third respectively, decide to dissolve partnership at 31st Dec., 19...

The Balance Sheet of the firm at that date is as below—

BALANCE SHEET
AS AT 31ST DECEMBER, 19..

	£			£
Capital—		Premises . . .		2,500
Dixon	4,000	Fittings		500
Matthews . . .	1,000	Stock		4,000
Creditors	3,600	Debtors		1,200
		Cash		400
	£8,600			£8,600

The Premises and Fittings were disposed of for £2,600; the stock fetched at auction £2,000, the debtors realized £1,140. The creditors were paid off. The expenses of realization amounted to £150.

Prepare the accounts to show the realization in the books of the firm.

EXERCISE 55

M. Ash and T. Rowan, independent sole traders, decided to amalgamate their businesses as from 1st January, 19.., and to trade in partnership thereafter under the firm name of Ash, Rowan, and Company. Their Balance Sheets as at the date of amalgamation were as below—

M. ASH'S BALANCE SHEET

	£		£
Capital	9,600	Freehold Property . .	1,400
Creditors	1,100	Furniture and Fittings .	400
		Stock	5,000
		Debtors . . .	3,000
		Cash at Bank . .	900
	£10,700		£10,700

T. ROWAN'S BALANCE SHEET

	£		£
Capital	3,200	Furniture and Fittings .	200
Creditors . . .	1,260	Stock	3,000
Bank Overdraft . . .	240	Debtors	1,500
	£4,700		£4,700

The partnership firm took over all the assets and liabilities as shown, subject to the following adjustments: Both stocks were reduced in value by 10 per cent: Rowan wrote off a debtor's account for £200 as bad and the Goodwill of Ash's business was valued at £2,000 which was credited to Ash.

Draw up the initial Balance Sheet of the partnership firm.

EXERCISE 56

Below are the Balance Sheets of two sole traders who have agreed to amalgamate their businesses as from 1st January, 19...

B. QUICK'S BALANCE SHEET

	£		£
Capital	7,000	Freehold Premises .	2,000
Creditors . . .	2,500	Furniture and Fittings .	400
Bills Payable . . .	800	Stock . . .	4,000
		Debtors . . .	3,000
		Bills Receivable . .	500
		Cash at Bank . .	400
	£10,300		£10,300

B. SLOW'S BALANCE SHEET

	£		£
Capital	4,500	Freehold Premises .	1,400
Creditors . . .	1,400	Furniture and Fittings .	350
Bills Payable . . .	250	Stock . . .	2,800
		Debtors . . .	1,000
		Cash at Bank . .	600
	£6,150		£6,150

The firm is to take over all the liabilities and assets at the values shown in the respective Balance Sheets except that a provision for bad debts is to be raised at 5 per cent, Quick's stock is to be reduced by 10 per cent and Goodwill is to be taken into account, Quick's £2,000, Slow's £1,000.

Prepare the opening Balance Sheet of the partnership.

EXERCISE 57

X and Y are independent traders in the same line of business, their respective Balance Sheets on 31st December, 19.., being as follows—

X BALANCE SHEET

AS AT 31ST DECEMBER, 19..

	£		£
Capital	22,400	Goodwill . . .	2,000
Sundry Creditors . .	2,047	Freehold Property .	2,400
		Fixtures and Fittings .	530
		Stock . . .	10,854
		Debtors . . .	7,591
		Cash at Bank . .	1,072
	£24,447		£24,447

Y BALANCE SHEET

AS AT 31ST DECEMBER, 19..

	£		£
Capital	4,660	Fixtures and Fittings .	180
Bills Payable . . .	1,200	Stock . . .	5,171
Sundry Creditors . .	2,318	Debtors . . .	3,146
Bank Overdraft . .	319		
	£8,497		£8,497

X and Y decided to amalgamate their businesses as from 1st January, 19.., the firm taking over all the assets and liabilities at the figures stated except Y's Fixtures and Fittings, which he was to retain and dispose of, and Y's Stock which is to be written down by £280. The Goodwill of Y's business was agreed to be valued at £600.

Draw up the opening Balance Sheet of the partnership.

(R.S.A.)

CHAPTER XI

LIMITED LIABILITY COMPANIES

THE accounts considered hitherto have been those of sole traders and partnerships, and the trading records have been shown as similar under both forms of business ownership. The purpose now is to consider, as another form of ownership, the limited liability company. Again the trading records in the books of account will not differ from those kept by a sole trader or by partners. It is the records of ownership that will differ in company accounts, just as the accounts of a partnership differed from those of a sole trader in these particulars.

A company is an association of persons sanctioned by Act of Parliament to become a corporate body for a special purpose. In a partnership the members are themselves the firm, but the incorporation of a company gives to it a legal personality separate from the persons composing it. In an action in the courts of law the company is sued upon and may sue in its own name, whereas a partnership is not a person in law distinct from the partners themselves.

The law relating to companies is contained in the Companies Act, 1948. The first Companies Act was passed in 1855 and there were many subsequent Acts, but the Act of 1948 consolidates the earlier Acts and contains the provisions now in force.

Private Companies

The companies referred to in this and subsequent chapters are public companies. Many companies, however, are private companies. The essential differences are: (a) that two persons (as against seven) are sufficient as the minimum number to form a private company, (b) that the private company must restrict the right to transfer its shares, (c) that it prohibits any invitation to the public to subscribe towards its capital, and (d) limits the number of its members to fifty, excluding members who are employees or were employees on acquiring shares.

Private companies are popular as a form of ownership for the owner of a business can thereby avoid the risk of unlimited liability attaching to a sole trading concern or partnership, yet still keep the control of the business in his hands.

The accounts of a private company do not differ in form from those of a public company.

Formation of a Company

The Act provides that any seven or more persons may form a public company, and any two or more a private company, provided that they apply to the Registrar of Companies and comply with the requirements of the Act.

The application must be in writing, and the document used is called the Memorandum of Association. The Memorandum must be signed by each of the applicants, who must also write opposite his name the number of shares he takes.

The Act stipulates that the Memorandum must contain the following information—

1. The name of the Company, with the word "Limited" as the last word of its name.
2. Where the registered office is situated.
3. The objects for which the company is formed.
4. That the liability of the members is limited.
5. The amount of the share capital with which the company proposes to be registered, and the division thereof into shares of a fixed amount.

Another document is usually prepared setting out the regulations regarding the transfer of shares in the company, the holding of meetings, and other matters of internal organization. This is called the Articles of Association. If a company does not prepare these regulations then it must abide by the regulations contained in the first schedule to the Companies Act, 1948, which is known as "Table A."

The Memorandum and Articles of Association, duly stamped for stamp duty and fees, and accompanied by certain other forms, are left with the Registrar of Companies who, if all is in order, shortly issues a Certificate of Incorporation. The company is now formed and those who signed the Memorandum are its first members. The documents are filed with the Registrar of Companies, and may be inspected by the public at Bush House, London, and at Parliament Square, Edinburgh, on payment of a small fee.

Company's Name and Office

A company will not be registered with a name identical with one already in existence, nor may it be registered with a name which in the opinion of the Board of Trade is undesirable. Except for companies formed for charitable purposes, etc., the last word of the name chosen must be "Limited."

A company must register the address of its office with the Registrar of Companies and give notice of any change. The registered office is the address for all notices and communications, and every company must have its name affixed or painted outside every office or place in which its business is carried on, and must mention its name in all notices, advertisements, and other official publications of the company, and in all bills of exchange, cheques, orders for money or goods, invoices and receipts.

Objects of the Company

These must be set out in the Memorandum of Association, and a company cannot legally do any business other than that covered by this clause.

Share Capital

The capital proposed for the company must be mentioned in the Memorandum of Association. The amount will depend upon the nature of the business and the capital required for its development. The Act further requires the capital sum to be divided into shares of a fixed amount. If the capital is registered as £100,000, then this sum may be divided into 100,000 fixed amounts of £1 each or, say, 400,000 of £0·25 each or 20,000 of £5 each. Each such fixed amount is called a share in the capital of the company. The £1 share is most commonly used. It is the number of such shares he takes that a subscriber to the Memorandum must write opposite to his name when signing the Memorandum of Association.

After the company is incorporated it may appeal to the public (unless a private company) to contribute to its capital, that is, to invite them to become shareholders. Such shareholders are members of the company, and there is no statutory limit to the number of shareholders a public company may have except that its authorized (or registered) share capital must not be exceeded. This is in contrast to a partnership as, by Sections 429 and 434 of the Companies Act, 1948, the members of a partnership may not exceed twenty in number, and the membership is limited to ten if the partnership intends to carry on the business of banking.

The offer of shares to the public is made by the issue of a prospectus setting out particulars of the company and its shares and the offer, with all relevant details, together with a form of application for the shares. Copies of these prospectuses are often published as advertisements in the daily newspapers.

Member's Liability

The Memorandum must state that the liability of the members is limited. Such liability refers to the debts or losses of the company, and a shareholder is not liable for these beyond the amount of share capital he has contributed or agreed to contribute.

If the shareholder agreed to contribute £10 by taking up ten £1 shares, then his loss, if any, would be limited to £10. This is again in contrast to the liability of the partners in a partnership firm whose liability extends beyond their share in the partnership to the whole extent of their private property.

It is this principle of limited liability (first introduced by the Companies Act of 1855) that has made companies so popular as a form of business ownership. Many are willing to take up shares in an enterprise in which the limit of possible loss is known, who would be unwilling to venture if the smallest contribution made them liable to the whole extent of their possessions.

Dividends

The profits of a company are shared between the members according to their holdings of share capital, and this distribution of profits is known as the payment of dividends. The Articles of Association usually contain the rules for payment, and these take into consideration the classes of shares into which the company's capital is divided.

Classes of Shares

The share capital of a company may be divided into different classes of shares. Most companies have but one, two, or three classes of shares. Heavily capitalized concerns may have very many kinds. The commonest classes are (a) Preference Shares, (b) Ordinary Shares, (c) Deferred Shares. The basis of classification is the order in which the members have the right to share in the profits of the company.

(a) PREFERENCE SHARES. These are entitled to a first share in the profits of the company. As other classes of shares will rank for dividend after the Preference shares, the latter bear a fixed dividend on their face value, e.g. 5 per cent. Preference shares may also have a prior claim for the repayment of capital should the company go into liquidation. This right, however, depends upon the terms of issue.

(b) ORDINARY SHARES. These form the largest class of shares in limited companies, and are usually entitled to the surplus profits after the Preference shares have been satisfied.

(c) DEFERRED SHARES. When this class of shares exists, the dividend going to the Ordinary shares is fixed and the

Examples

(*a*) *Builders, Ltd.*, has share capital of £100,000 divided into 100,000 Ordinary shares of £1 each.

Profit for the year available for dividend = £20,000.

Dividend on Ordinary shares = 20 per cent or £0·20 per £1 share.

(*b*) *Carpenters, Ltd.*, has share capital of £100,000 divided into 50,000 5 per cent Preference shares of £1 each and 50,000 Ordinary shares of £1 each.

Profit for the year available for dividend = £20,000.

Then, dividend on 50,000 5 per cent £1 Preference shares = £2,500.

Surplus of £17,500 is available for Ordinary shares, i.e. £17,500 on 50,000 £1 Ordinary shares = 35 per cent or £0·35 per £1 share.

(*c*) *Plasterers, Ltd.*, has share capital of £100,000 divided into 25,000 5 per cent Preference shares of £1 each, 50,000 Ordinary shares of £1 each, and 25,000 Deferred shares of £1 each. The Deferred shares are entitled to the surplus profits after payment of 10 per cent per annum on the Ordinary shares.

Profit for the year available for dividend = £20,000.

Dividend on 25,000 5 per cent Preference shares = £1,250.

Ten per cent dividend on 50,000 Ordinary shares = £5,000.

Surplus available for Deferred shares = £13,750, i.e. 55 per cent or £0·55 per £1 share.

Deferred shares become entitled to the surplus profits after the Preference and Ordinary shares have been satisfied.

There are many variations from the above classes of shares, and some of the more important are mentioned below. It will be seen that they depend upon the order in which the dividend is payable and the limitation of the amount. All, of course, depend upon there being a profit available for dividend.

Preference shares may be *cumulative* or *non-cumulative*. Should the profits be insufficient to meet the dividend on the Preference shares, then, should they be cumulative, the right to dividend accumulates or mounts up from year to year, and no dividend on other classes may be paid until the arrears of dividend and the current year's claim have been met.

Preference shares are usually designated cumulative or non-cumulative, but if they are not specifically described as non-cumulative, the Preference shareholders are entitled to assume that they are, in fact, cumulative.

Holders of non-cumulative Preference shares are not entitled to payment of arrears of dividend in future years should the profits in any year be insufficient to meet their dividend.

PARTICIPATING PREFERENCE SHARES. This class of share has the right to participate or share further in the surplus profits remaining after the payment of the fixed preferential dividend, and of a fixed dividend on the Ordinary and other shares.

For example, the Preference shares may be entitled to share equally with the Ordinary shares in the remaining profits after payment of the Preference share dividend and, say, 15 per cent on the Ordinary share capital.

PREFERRED ORDINARY SHARES. These are entitled to a fixed dividend after payment of the Preference shares dividend, and before the division of profits to the Ordinary shareholders.

REDEEMABLE PREFERENCE SHARES. The Companies Act, 1948, permits a company, duly authorized in its Articles, to issue Preference shares which may be redeemed, that is, the capital sum returned to the holders of such shares. Such redemption must be made out of profits or out of the proceeds of a fresh issue of shares. The profits may be accumulated year by year for this purpose, but must be placed to a special "Capital Redemption Reserve Fund".

The issuing of these various classes of shares is a financial expedient designed to encourage investment by all types of investors. Some persons are attracted by the greater security of dividend and market value attaching to Preference shares. Others prefer the possibility of larger dividends and, therefore, will turn more readily to the Ordinary shares. Participating Preference shares offer both the advantage of priority of payment of dividend and the opportunity to share in the surplus profits.

CHAPTER XII

LIMITED LIABILITY COMPANIES:
THE ISSUE OF SHARES

A LIMITED company may be formed to acquire an existing business or to start a new concern. In either case the new company will need persons to manage its commercial activities, and to be responsible for the carrying out of the requirements of the Companies Act and other details of organization. In sole-trading and partnership concerns all the members of the firm are usually engaged in managing the business, but the members of a company may number hundreds and, in some cases, thousands, so that the managing function is delegated by the owners (i.e. shareholders) to a group of persons known collectively as the Board of Directors of the company. Under Sect. 176 of the Companies Act, 1948, a public company must have at least two directors, and it is usual for four or five to be appointed. In large companies the Board may consist of ten or twenty directors to whom special duties are delegated. Directors are usually remunerated by fees for the work done for the company. Such fees are authorized by the Articles of Association and, normally, a director must hold shares in the company.

Appointment of Directors

The number of the directors of a company and who shall be the first directors are matters frequently determined by the signatories to the Memorandum of Association. Such determination is by all or the majority of the signatories signing a formal statement to that effect. In other cases the first directors may be mentioned by name in the Articles of Association. The directors usually have power to fill casual vacancies,

and the Articles of Association usually provide that one or more
of the directors shall retire annually, but shall be eligible for
re-election. Or their places may be filled by others, as decided
by the members in general meeting.

The Issue of Shares

One of the first acts of the directors will be the consideration
of the offer of the company's share capital for public subscription. This will involve the preparation and issue of a "prospectus" setting out the offer and many particulars of the
company. A copy must be signed and dated by the directors,
and filed with the Registrar of Companies on or before the
date of publication. Sects. 38 and 39 of the Companies Act,
1948, together with the fourth schedule, set out at length the
strict requirements of the law regarding the contents of a
prospectus, and great care must be exercised in preparation of
the document, as it is the basis of the contract between the
company and the shareholder. Misrepresentation of fact in
the prospectus entitles a shareholder, who relied in good faith
upon the prospectus, to take action at law for revision of his
contract to take the shares.

The prospectus must contain, among other things, a copy
of the contents of the company's Memorandum of Association.
This does not apply to the abridged prospectus seen as advertisements in the daily Press, but such abridged prospectuses
are valuable material for study by the student of company law
and accounts.

APPLICATION FORM. Each prospectus contains an application form for shares. The Press advertised prospectuses have
a similar form printed at the foot. The applicant fills in the
required particulars and sends the form, together with the
amount payable on application, to the company's bankers.

The next steps taken by the company are briefly as follows.
At the end of the period during which the subscription list is
open the company obtains the application forms from its
banker, and checks the amounts stated thereon with the
entries in the bank pass book. The total number of shares

applied for is then known, and will be either more or less than the full amount offered to the public. If the issue was of 100,000 shares of £1 each and the public applied for 70,000 shares only, the issue is said to be "under-subscribed." It would be "over-subscribed" if the applications amounted to more than 100,000 shares. As the maximum offered is 100,000 shares, the applicants, in the case of over-subscription, cannot be given all the shares they have applied for. Usually the applications are reduced *pro rata* so that the total will not be exceeded, and each applicant gets a similar proportion of his original application.

ALLOTMENT. The decision of the directors to allot the shares is known as "going to allotment." Allotment sheets are prepared showing the names and addresses of the applicants, the number of shares allotted to each applicant, and the balance of money due on the shares allotted. The directors pass a resolution that the shares be allotted in accordance with this list, and this is recorded in the minutes of meeting.

No allotment, however, may be made unless the minimum subscription towards the issue has been secured. This minimum must be stated in the prospectus, and is the amount which, in the directors' opinion, is the least that will provide for the property, if any, proposed to be purchased, for the preliminary expenses of formation of the company and leave sufficient working capital.

ALLOTMENT LETTERS. A letter is posted to each applicant to whom shares have been allotted, stating the number of shares allotted, the amount paid towards the value of the shares, and the amount due upon allotment, together with a request that this amount be paid forthwith.

The posting of the allotment letter is the acceptance by the company of the applicant's offer to take shares, and the contract between the company and the applicant is then complete, so that the balance owing on the shares becomes a debt due to the company.

LETTER OF REGRET. If no allotment of shares is made to an applicant a letter is sent regretting that no allotment has been made, and enclosing a cheque for the refund of the application money.

RETURN OF ALLOTMENTS. The company must, within one month after allotment, make a return of allotments to the Registrar of Companies. The return must state the number and nominal amount of the shares comprised in the allotment, and the names, addresses, and descriptions of the allottees, together with the amount paid or due and payable on each share. This return must bear a £0·25 stamp, the fee for registration of the document.

The Capital of a Company

As mentioned earlier, the Memorandum of Association must state the amount of the share capital with which the company proposes to be registered, and the division thereof into shares of a fixed amount. The amount of capital so stated is known as the *authorized* or *registered capital* of the company. Sometimes, also, it is called the *nominal* capital.

The directors may decide to offer all or part only of the authorized capital to the public for subscription. The amount offered is called the *issued capital*. The public may take up all the shares offered for subscription, or only a part. The amount subscribed for is the *subscribed capital* of the company, which may or may not coincide in amount with either the issued or authorized capital.

When an issue of shares is made it is usual to provide for payment by instalments. An amount will be payable on application. By Sect. 47 of the Companies Act, 1948, this first instalment must not be less than 5 per cent of the nominal value of the share. A second instalment is due on allotment of the shares. The allotment letter which informs the applicant that he has been allotted shares also requests payment of this second instalment forthwith.

Subsequent instalments (if any) to complete the payment are at future dates according to the decision of the directors; possibly one month after allotment.

These later instalments are known as *calls* from the fact

that, at due date, the shareholders are called upon to pay the sum due. Notification is sent out in the form of a call letter.

That part of the subscribed capital which has been called up is known as the *called-up capital*, and the amount actually paid of the called-up capital is known as the *paid-up capital* of the company. When all the instalments are paid the shares are described as *fully-paid shares*. There are, however, cases when instalments are not met at due date, and the *calls* are *in arrear*. The called-up capital and paid-up capital may not for this reason always coincide in amount. Another reason may be that the directors have decided not to call up the full amount, leaving, say £0·25 per share uncalled. This uncalled capital is a liability of the shareholders which they may be called upon to meet at any time. Under Sect. 60 of the Act, however, a company may, by special resolution, determine that the uncalled capital shall not be capable of being called up except in the event of the company being wound up. Such uncalled portion of the share capital is then of the nature of a reserve fund.

The following is an illustration of the different kinds of capital of a company—

Masters and Men, Ltd., whose registered capital is £100,000 divided into 100,000 shares of £1 each, offered 60,000 shares for public subscription payable as follows—
20p. per share on application.
30p. per share on allotment.
25p. per share one month after allotment.
25p. per share two months later.
The issued capital was fully subscribed and all the application and allotment money and the first call and final call were received with the exception of the final call of 25p. on 1,000 shares which is still owing by a shareholder.

On these assumptions the capital of the company may be summarized as below—

	£
Authorized, Nominal or Registered Capital .	100,000
Subscribed Capital	60,000
Issued Capital	60,000
Called-up Capital	60,000
Paid-up Capital	59,750
Calls in arrear	250

In this example there is no uncalled capital.

Calls in Advance

In the above example a shareholder may have decided to pay the final call of 30p. per share at the time of paying the first call. He has then paid the call in advance, and it is usual to provide in the Articles of Association that interest shall be paid on such calls in advance as they are really loans to the company until the date the call is actually due for payment. Such interest is a debt due from the company to the shareholder, and is payable whether profits are made or not.

Distinctive Numbers

Sect. 74 of the Act provides that each share in a company having a share capital shall be distinguished by its appropriate number. Where, however, all the shares of a company or all the shares of a particular class are fully paid, numbers may be dispensed with.

Share Certificates

Each shareholder is given a certificate (usually signed by two directors and the secretary and bearing the seal of the company) which is commonly worded as below—

"This is to certify that Henry Masters of Claremont Park, Windsor, is the registered proprietor of One thousand shares of £1 each, fully paid, numbered 501 to 1500 inclusive, in Masters and Men, Limited, pursuant to the Memorandum and Articles of Association of the said Company."

Unless the conditions of issue of the shares provide otherwise, every company must have the share certificates complete and ready for delivery within two months after the allotment of the shares. The certificates are handed over in exchange for the allotment letter and the receipts for the subsequent instalments.

The Transfer of Shares

A shareholder cannot obtain at will the return of capital invested in a company. Should the investment be in redeemable Preference shares the capital is returnable at the redemption date according to the terms of issue. The capital value of other shares may be returned by a company, after certain formalities, if it finds that its capital is in excess of its requirements owing to some happening lessening its trading possibilities. Apart from these two instances, which are at the option of the company and not of the shareholder, a member can only realize the value of his shares by the sale of them to another person. He may sell all or part of his holding, but he must first find his purchaser.

A Stock Exchange is a market for the sale and purchase of shares and other securities, and shares may be sold on the Exchange through the services of a stockbroker. But not all companies have their shares included in the Stock Exchange list of shares dealt in. Certain rules and formalities are imposed by the Stock Exchange before the facility is granted. For many companies the dealings in their shares are not sufficiently numerous, and the shareholder must seek a purchaser elsewhere than on a Stock Exchange. Often another shareholder is found willing to increase his holding, but if the company's prospects are not bright it may be difficult, and is sometimes impossible, to find a purchaser.

On sale the shareholder can obtain only the market value of his shares. He may have subscribed one pound for each of his £1 shares, but when he sells the share he can get only what the purchaser is willing to give. This may be a pound a share. It may be more or less than a pound a share. The purchaser will take into consideration the standing of the company, the dividends paid in past years, and the prospects, as far as they can be estimated, of dividends in the future. However, whether the purchaser pays £0·25 or £4·25 for a £1 share, the company is not concerned, but simply records that the seller has parted with a £1 share bearing a certain number, and the purchaser is now the holder in the seller's place.

Shares may be sold even if not fully paid up. The purchaser becomes liable for the outstanding calls, and in every case assumes all the rights and obligations of the former holder.

Every transfer of shares must be in writing (Sect. 75), and

in prescribed form. It is usual to purchase a common form of transfer from a law stationer. The transfer form is signed by the seller and handed over to the purchaser, together with the share certificate, in exchange for cash. The purchaser must have the transfer stamped for duty. After signature by the purchaser, the latter lodges the certificate and transfer with the company and pays the transfer fee, usually 15p. A new certificate is prepared by the company, delivery of which to the purchaser must be made within two months from the lodging of the transfer.

Transfer fees are a minor source of profit to the company, and are credited to a Transfer Fees Account for eventual transfer to the credit side of the Profit and Loss Account.

Stock

As explained above, the capital of a company is divided into equal shares or parts, and each such share may bear a distinctive number. Under Sect. 62 of the Act a company may convert any shares into stock and, if it so wishes, reconvert such stock into shares. Such shares must, before conversion, be fully paid.

A company having £100,000 capital dividend into 100,000 shares of £1 each, fully paid, may decide to convert the shares into stock. The capital then becomes, not, as it was, an aggregate of 100,000 separate parts of £1 each, but, in effect, a mass or block of capital of £100,000. The holder of 500 £1 shares then possesses, not separate £1 shares, but a £500 piece of the total mass of £100,000 capital.

The stock is transferable by the same process as are shares, but most companies stipulate that transfers must be units of, say, £5 or multiples thereof. Some stocks may be transferable in fractions of a pound so that the holder may sell, for example £140·50 of his holding. The market value of stock is quoted at so much for each £100 of stock, whereas shares are quoted at the market value for one share.

CHAPTER XIII

LIMITED LIABILITY COMPANIES: STATUTORY BOOKS

A COMPANY is bound by law to keep proper books of account in which must be recorded all sums of money received and expended, all sales and purchases of goods and its assets and liabilities.

In addition to these records of its business activities, a company is also required by law to keep certain other statutory books.

These are—

Register of Members and an Index (where necessary).
Minute Book.
Register of Directors and Secretaries.
Register of Mortgages and Charges.
Register of Directors' Shareholdings.

The Register of Members

Every company must keep in one or more books and enter therein (under Sect. 110)—

(*a*) The names and addresses of its members, a statement of the shares held by each member, distinguishing each share by its number as long as the share has a number, and of the amount paid, or agreed to be considered as paid, on the shares of each member.

(*b*) The date at which each person was entered in the register as a member.

(*c*) The date at which any person ceased to be a member.

If the company has more than fifty members, it must keep an index of the names of the members unless the Register of Members is in such a form as to constitute in itself an index.

The index may be a card index, and all necessary alterations must be made within fourteen days.

The Register of Members and index are usually kept at the registered office, and must be open for inspection for not less than two hours in each business day by members without charge, and by any other person on payment of one shilling or any less sum prescribed by the company.

The company may, on giving notice by advertisement, close the register for not exceeding thirty days in each year, and it is usual for a company to close it for fourteen days prior to its Annual General Meeting. The closure means that no change of ownership of shares will be recorded during the period, and this allows for the preparation of the dividend lists.

Separate registers are kept of Ordinary shareholders, Preference shareholders, etc., where different classes of shares are issued.

Generally the Register of Members is combined with the Share Ledger (to which fuller reference is made later), and books suitably ruled may be purchased from company or law stationers.

Minute Books

A company must keep minutes of all proceedings of its general meetings of shareholders and of all proceedings at meetings of its directors or of its managers in books kept for that purpose, and, where signed by the chairman of the meeting or of the next succeeding meeting, such minutes are evidence of the proceedings.

The minutes of the general meetings of shareholders may de inspected without charge by members, and a copy of any minutes must be supplied to members on demand at a charge of not exceeding $2\frac{1}{2}$p. for every hundred words (Sect. 113).

Register of Directors and Secretaries

Every company must keep a register of its directors and secretaries containing, in the case of directors, their names in full, residential address, nationality, occupation, other directorships and, for public companies, their age. They must also send to the Registrar of Companies notification of any change of directors or particulars within fourteen days of the change happening (Sect. 200).

Register of Mortgages and Charges

Mortgages are referred to in Chapter XIV. Every mortgage or charge affecting the company's property or business must be registered with the Registrar or Companies, and a full record kept by the company in its Register of Mortgages and Charges, and all releases from such charges must also be notified to the Registrar (Sects. 96, 98 104).

Register of Directors' Shareholdings

Every company must keep a register showing particulars of directors' shareholdings, etc., as provided for by Sect. 195 of the Act.

In addition to the above a company finds it necessary to keep certain other books, so that its record may be complete and easily dealt with. Some of these other books are the Register of Transfers, Register of Probates of deceased members' estates, and the Agenda Book for directors' meetings in which the secretary sets down the business to be transacted and the chairman makes his notes. The Agenda Book provides the material for the preparation of the minutes of meeting.

Annual Return

Every company having a share capital must once a year, subject to the exceptions laid down in Sect. 124, make a return of all persons who are members of the company, and of all persons who ceased to be members since the date of the last return.

The return must state the names and addresses of all the past or present members mentioned in it and the shares held by each, specifying shares transferred since the last return and the date of registration of transfer.

The Return must also state the address of the registered office, or if the Register of Members or any other register is kept elsewhere, then the address of the office at which it is kept, and full details of the company's capital in accordance with the requirements of Sect. 124 and the sixth schedule of the Act. Except in the case of exempt private companies a copy of the last Balance Sheet signed by a director and the secretary must be forwarded with the Annual Return (Sect. 127). An exempt private company is a private company in which no other company has an interest and in which no person other than the holder has an interest in the shares. Copies of the Summary of Capital and Annual Return suitable for use may be purchased for a few pence from law stationers.

The Return must be completed within forty-two days of the annual general meeting (Sect. 126) and forwarded to the Registrar of Companies, signed by a Director and the Secretary.

CHAPTER XIV

COMPANY ACCOUNTS:
THE ISSUE OF CAPITAL, DEBENTURE ISSUES

THE following example will serve to illustrate the chief variations in the form of accounts caused by a business concern
being owned by a limited company.

Example

Raymond's, Limited, whose authorized capital is 150,000 Ordinary
shares of £1 each, offered 100,000 shares for public subscription on 1st July
payable as follows—

15p. per share on application.
35p. ,, ,, ,, allotment.
25p. ,, ,, one month after allotment.
25p. ,, ,, one month later.

All shares were subscribed for and allotted and the instalments paid at
due dates with the exception of the final call of 25p. per share on 1,000
shares which is still outstanding.

The first happening is the receipt of the application money.
Within a few days the instalment due on allotment will also
be received. These sums will be received by the company's
bankers and will be placed to the credit of the company. The
company will record details of the applications and of the
applicants in a special book—the Application and Allotment
Book. The application money received will be entered on the
debit side of the Cash Book and credited to the Application
and Allotment Account in the Ledger.

Similar entries will be made when the instalments due on
allotment are received.

The entries for the first two instalments in the above illustration will, therefore, appear as given on page 102.

Dr.   CASH BOOK   **Cr.**

		£		Payments		£

July 1	*Receipts*
	To Application
	   and Allotment
	   (Sundry
	   amounts
	   received on
	   application .
				Payments		

		15,000				

8	,, Application
	   and Allotment
	   (Sundry
	   amounts
	   received on
	   allotment) .					

		35,000				

Dr.   APPLICATION AND ALLOTMENT   **Cr.**

		£					£

			July 1	By Cash
				   (Application
				   money) .
					.	CB	15,000

			8	,, Cash
				   (Allotment
				   money) .
					.	CB	35,000

It has been mentioned already that the applicants are not shareholders until the act of allotment by the directors takes place. After the posting of the allotment letter the applicants then become liable to the company for the remaining instalments on their shares. Until allotment the company has no Capital Account proper, and the money received from the applicants is placed to a temporary Application and Allotment Account as above. On allotment a Share Capital Account is opened in the Ledger, and the transfer is made by Journal entry to this account from the Application and Allotment Account. The latter account is then closed.

JOURNAL

		£	£
July 5	Application and Allotment . . *Dr.* To Ordinary Share Capital . . Being 15p. on application and 35p. on allot- ment on 100,000 Ordinary shares allotted by resolution of Directors dated 5th July, 19...	50,000	50,000

Dr.					APPLICATION AND ALLOTMENT			Cr.
July 5	To Ordinary Share Capital	.	J	£ 50,000	July 1	By Cash (Application money) .	CB	£ 15,000
					8	,, Cash (Allotment money) .	CB	35,000
				£50,000				£50,000

Dr.			ORDINARY SHARE CAPITAL			Cr.
		£	July 5	By Application and Allotment	J	£ 50,000

There is now a capital Account in the financial books of the company. It is, however, a single account representing the capital liability of the business to all its part owners, who may be numerous. Shareholders, having put money into the business, should each have a separate account. They have such separate Capital Accounts in the Share Ledger. The Register of Members which a company must keep by law is usually so ruled that it contains a Share Account for each member. This is more convenient for reference and for working than to have the private Ledger overloaded with numerous individual Capital Accounts. The above Ordinary Share Capital Account is therefore a summary account, the financial position of each shareholder in relation to the company being entered in the combined Register of Members and Share Ledger.

The First Call Account

The first call is due, in this example, one month after allotment. The shareholders will be notified by the issue of a call letter.

On a call being due a Call Account is opened and is debited with the amount due from the shareholders, and the Share Capital Account is credited with the like sum.

The Journal entry would be—

JOURNAL

Aug. 5	First Call Account . . . . . Dr.
	    To Ordinary Share Capital . . .
	Being a first call of 25p. per share on 100,000
	    Ordinary shares according to conditions
	    of issue.
			£
			25,000
				£
				
				25,000

As the call money is received the record will be made in
the Cash Book and the Call Account. The First Call Account,
to which the above Journal entries and, later, the Cash Book
will be posted, will appear as below—

Dr.			ORDINARY SHARE CAPITAL			Cr.
		£	July 5	By Application and Allotment	J	£ 50,000
			Aug. 5	,,　First Call .	J	25,000

Dr.			CASH BOOK			Cr.

July 1	*Receipts*
	To Application
	  and Allotment
	  (Sundry
	  amounts
	  received
	  on application)
		£		*Payments*		£

8	,, Application
	  and Allotment
	  (Sundry
	  amounts
	  received on
	  allotment) .
		12,500				

Aug. 8	,, Sundry
	  amounts—
	  being first call
	  of 25p. per
	  share . .
		37,500
		
		25,000				

Dr.			FIRST CALL			Cr.
Aug. 5	To Ordinary Share Capital .	£ 25,000	Aug. 8	By Cash . .	CB	£ 25,000

The Second and Final Call

Similar procedure will take place for this call as for the first call. On the call being made the Final Call Account will be debited and the Share Capital Account credited with the full amount. It is assumed, in this illustration, that a shareholder fails to pay the final call on 1,000 shares. This will appear in the Final Call Account as shown below.

JOURNAL

			£	£
Sept. 5	Final Call . . . . . *Dr.*		25,000	
	To Ordinary Share Capital . .			25,000
	Being final call of 25p. per share on 100,000 Ordinary shares according to conditions of issue.			

Dr.	ORDINARY SHARE CAPITAL							*Cr.*
			£	July 5	By Application and Allotment	J	50,000	£
				Aug. 5	,, First Call .	J	25,000	
				Sept. 5	,, Final Call	J	25,000	
							£100,000	

Dr.	CASH BOOK					*Cr.*
	Receipts	£		*Payments*		£
July 1	To Application and Allotment (Sundry amounts received on application) .	12,500				
8	,, Application and Allotment (Sundry amounts received on allotment) .	37,500				
Aug. 8	,, Sundry amounts— being first call of 25p. per share .	25,000				
Sept. 8	,, Sundry amounts —being final call of 25 p. per share . .	24,750				

Dr.   FINAL CALL   *Cr.*

			£					£
Sept. 5	To Ordinary Share Capital .	J	25,000	Sept. 8	By Cash .	.	CB	24,750

Calls in arrear are debts due to the company, but the capital liability of the company to its shareholders is lessened by the amount of the calls not received. It is customary, therefore, to show the calls in arrear as a deduction from the issued capital on the left-hand side of the Balance Sheet, and not as a debtor. (See Balance Sheet, below).

A company having several kinds of share capital (e.g. Ordinary, Preference, etc.) would, on offering the capital for public subscription, proceed as above for each class of share, so that in the books there would be an Ordinary Share Capital Account, a Preference Share Capital Account, and so on for each class, together with separate Application and Allotment Accounts and Call Accounts.

The Balance Sheet of a Company

The capital of Raymonds, Ltd., would appear in the Balance Sheet as below—

BALANCE SHEET

(LEFT-HAND SIDE ONLY)

	£	£
Nominal Capital		
150,000 Ordinary shares of £1 each	150,000	
Issued Capital		
100,000 Ordinary shares of £1 each fully paid . .	100,000	
Less Calls in arrear	250	
		99,750

The points to note are that the nominal or authorized capital is shown in the Balance Sheet for information only, and that only the issued and paid-up capital enters into the effective money column.

Calls in Advance

As already discussed in an earlier chapter, a company usually takes power in its Articles of Association to receive calls in advance of the due date, and to pay interest on such advance payments. A shareholder may desire to take advantage of this, as it relieves him of the trouble of making periodical payments. If T. Jones, for example, applied for 1,000 £1 shares on which £0·75 had been called up and paid the full £1 per share, £250 would represent a call paid in advance of the due date. Jones would be recorded as a holder of 1,000 £1 shares £0·75 paid. The £250 is a loan to the company at interest until such time that the final call is made.

The £250 must be recorded in a Calls in Advance Account.

Dr.			CALLS IN ADVANCE			*Cr.*
		£	Jan. 1	By Cash— T. Jones . .	CB	250

When the call is made the loan will become a payment of the call on T. Jones's shares. The Calls in Advance Account is then closed by a debit entry. "To Share Capital Account —£250" and a corresponding entry is made to the credit of the Share Capital Account.

Pending the call being made the £250 is shown in the Balance Sheet on the left-hand side, "Calls in Advance, £250."

On the interest being due (e.g. half-yearly at 5 per cent) the following entries will be made in the Journal and posted to the respective accounts—

JOURNAL

		£ 6·25	£
July 1	Interest . . . . . *Dr.*	6·25	
	To T. Jones		6·25
	Being interest at 5 per cent on calls paid in advance for the half year.		

A cheque will be sent to T. Jones involving a credit entry in the Cash Book and a debit entry in T. Jones's Account, which will then be closed. The balance of the Interest Account will be transferred to the Profit and Loss Account in due course.

Issue of Shares at a Discount

It is lawful under Sect. 57 of the Companies Act, 1948, for a company to issue shares at a discount subject to the following restrictions—

The shares must be of a class already issued.

A resolution of the company in general meeting must be passed authorizing the issue at a discount, and such resolution must be sanctioned by the court.

The maximum discount must be stated in the resolution.

The issue cannot be made within one year of the date on which the company was entitled to commence business.

The shares must be issued within one month after the sanction of the court.

Particulars of the discount allowed must be stated in every prospectus and shown in the company's Balance Sheets until written off.

Assume, as an example, the issue of 100,000 £1 Ordinary shares at a discount of 5 per cent, the payments being made £0·25 on application, £0·25 on allotment, and £0·45 as first and final call one month after allotment. The entries for the applications and allotments will be as shown earlier in this chapter. The call of £0·45 per share will be treated as below—

JOURNAL

	£	£
Ordinary Shares Call . . . *Dr.*	45,000	
Discount on Ordinary shares . . *Dr.*	5,000	
To Ordinary Share Capital . .		50,000
Being first and final call of £0·45 per share on 100,000 Ordinary shares of £1 each and the 5 per cent discount.		

When fully posted to the Ledger there will be, in the case of shares issued at a discount, an additional account—

Dr.	DISCOUNT ON ORDINARY SHARES		Cr.
	£		£
To 5% discount on 100,000 £1 Ordinary shares .	5,000		

The new issue of £100,000 will be shown in full on the left-hand side of the Balance Sheet, and will be included in the full total of capital issued of this particular class of share. The "Discount on Ordinary Shares Account—£5,000" will be shown on the right-hand side of the Balance Sheet. It should be written off against profits as soon as possible.

Issue of Shares at a Premium

Power to issue shares at a discount may assist a company to obtain fresh capital during the time its existing shares are quoted at below par value. On the other hand, when the shares stand at above par, the company may consider it worth while to issue shares at a premium and so take advantage of the demand for its shares. Usually, existing shareholders are given preference in the allotment of such shares.

Example

Radio Clocks, Ltd., having an authorized capital of 250,000 £1 shares of which 200,000 shares had been issued and fully paid, decided to offer the remainder of 50,000 shares for public subscription at £1·25 per share, payable £0·25 per share on application and £1·00 per share, including the premium, on allotment. All the application and allotment money was received.

JOURNAL

		£	£
Application and Allotment . . *Dr.*		62,500	
To Share Capital			50,000
„ Premium on Shares . . .			12,000
Being £0·25 per share on application and £1·00 on allotment, including premium of £0·25 per share on 50,000 £1 shares allotted on resolution of Directors date....			

The items will be posted as usual, the additional account appearing as below—

Dr.				PREMIUM ON SHARES		Cr.
			£			£
				By Application and Allotment		12,500

The Premium on Shares Account will be shown as a separate item on the left-hand side of the Balance Sheet—

BALANCE SHEET
(LEFT-HAND SIDE ONLY)

	£	£
Nominal Capital		
250,000 shares of £1 each	250,000	
Issued Capital		
250,000 shares of £1 each fully paid . . .		250,000
Premium on Shares Account		12,500

The premium is usually treated as of the nature of a capital reserve, and is retained in the business as additional working capital.

Although the premium represents a profit made by the company, it cannot be credited to Profit and Loss Account. It *can* be used in writing off preliminary (or formation) expenses: in paying up unissued shares to be issued as fully-paid bonus shares: in writing off discount allowed on shares or debentures (Sect. 56).

Preliminary Expenses

Every company will incur certain expenses consequent upon its formation, e.g. cost of printing the prospectus, the memorandum and articles of association: cost of share certificates, the company seal, books of account and statutory registers:

legal and surveying fees, stamp duties, etc. All these charges, which can amount to a considerable sum, are debited to a Preliminary or Formation Expenses Account and are written off against profit during the early years of the life of the company. Any balance outstanding on the account will appear on the Balance Sheet among the fictitious assets.

Debentures

Companies may require additional cash resources at any time to finance special developments or to take advantage of trading opportunities. The cash may be obtained by loans from banks or individuals. Banks, however, do not encourage loans for long periods, and if considerable sums are required companies may resort to an issue of debentures. The company borrows money and gives to the lender or lenders a document, called a debenture, which contains particulars of the sum borrowed, the rate of interest payable, and the terms of repayment of the capital sum. Most debentures are mortgage debentures, that is, the document contains a charge upon certain properties of the company in favour of the debenture-holders, so that if the company does not carry out the conditions regarding repayment of capital and interest the holders have the right to deal with the property charged to reimburse themselves.

It is essential to note that debentures represent loans to the company. The interest is a debt due to the debenture-holders, and is payable whether profits have been made or not. Outstanding interest must be provided for before profits are distributed. Debenture interest is usually paid half-yearly, and the student should look to see that all the interest has been paid or provided for. It is not infrequent to find the second half-year's interest outstanding.

Debentures are generally of £100 each and, on issue, the capital sum is usually payable by instalments. The entries in the company books are similar to those for an issue of shares, though it must be borne in mind that a debenture-holder is not a member of the company, but only a creditor.

Debentures are, however, transferable, and the common form of transfer is used as for shares.

Example

A limited company offered on 1st January, 19.., 100 5 per cent debentures of £100 each payable as to £20 on application, £40 on allotment, and £40 on 1st March, 19... The full amount was subscribed and allotted and the final instalments paid on 1st March.

JOURNAL

		£	£
Jan. 6	Debentures Application and Allotment . . . . . *Dr.* To 5% Debentures . . . Being £20 on application and £40 on allotment on 100 5% Debentures on resolution of Directors dated 6th Jan., 19...	6,000	6,000
Mar. 1	Debentures Call . . . *Dr.* To 5% Debentures . . . Being final instalment of £40 on 100 5% Debentures.	4,000	4,000

Dr.				FIVE PER CENT DEBENTURES			*Cr.*
		£	Jan. 6	By Debentures Application and Allotment			£ 6,000
			Mar. 1	,, Debentures Call .			4,000

Dr.				DEBENTURE APPLICATION AND ALLOTMENT			*Cr.*
Jan. 6	To 5% Debentures .	£ 6,000	Jan. 6	By Cash .	.	CB	£ 6,000

Dr.				CALL ON DEBENTURES			*Cr.*
Mar 1	To 5% Debentures .	£ 4,000	Mar. 1	By Cash .	.	CB	£ 4,000

Dr. <div style="text-align:center">CASH BOOK</div> *Cr.*

		£				£
Jan. 6	To Debentures Application and Allotment	6,000				
Mar. 1	,, Debenture Call	4,000				

The total of the debenture issue appears on the left-hand side of the Balance Sheet next below the share capital.

Debentures Issued at a Premium

In the above example the debentures are offered at par. The price of each £100 debenture is £100. Debentures may, however, be issued at a premium or at a discount. If the standing of the company issuing the debentures is good, so that the security is a sound investment, the company may take full advantage of this and offer the £100 debentures at, say, £102 each, or, in other words, at a premium of £2 a debenture. The premium is not loan capital but of the nature of ordinary profits, but it is usual to treat it as a reserve of capital to be retained in the business, and it is shown separately as such on the left-hand side of the Balance Sheet.

Example

A limited company offered for subscription on 1st January, 19.., 1,000 5 per cent debentures of £100 each at the price of £102 (or at a premium of £2 per debenture), payable £32 on application (including the premium) and the balance (£70) on allotment. The issue was duly subscribed and allotted and the money received.

JOURNAL

		£	£
Jan. 6	Debentures Application and Allotment . . . . . *Dr.* To 5% Debentures . . . ,, Debentures Premium . Being £32 on application and £70 on allotment per debenture on resolution of Directors dated 6th January.	102,000	100,000 2,000

Dr.			FIVE PER CENT DEBENTURES			Cr.
		£	Jan. 6	By Debentures Application and Allotment		£ 100,000

Dr.			DEBENTURE APPLICATION AND ALLOTMENT			Cr.
Jan. 6	To 5% Debentures . ,, Debentures Premium .	£ 100,000 2,000	Jan. 6	By Cash .		£ 102,000

Dr.			DEBENTURE PREMIUM			Cr.
		£	Jan. 6	By Application and Allotment		£ 2,000

Dr.			CASH BOOK			Cr.
Jan. 6	To Debenture Application and Allotment	£ 102,000				£

BALANCE SHEET
(LEFT-HAND SIDE ONLY)

	£
Share Capital	?
1,000 5% Debentures of £100 each	100,000
Premium on Debentures	2,000

Debentures Issued at a Discount

To encourage investors to take up a debenture issue it may be necessary to offer them a discount on the face value, so that a £100 debenture may be offered at a price of, say, £95. A company must be authorized by its Articles to issue debentures at a discount, and the discount is an actual loss. The company, however, is liable to the debenture-holder for

the full face value of each debenture, and must record this
liability for the full £100 in its books.

Example

A limited company offered 1,000 5 per cent debentures of £100 each for
subscription on 1st January, 19.., at a price of £95 each, payable £25 on
application, £40 on allotment, and £30 on 1st March, 19... The issue was
fully subscribed and allotment made on 6th January. All money was duly
received.

JOURNAL

Jan. 6	Debenture Application and Allotment . . . . . *Dr.*	65,000	
	To 5% Debentures		65,000
	Being £25 on application £40 on allotment on 1,000 debentures on resolution of Directors dated 6th January, 19...		
Mar. 1	Debentures Call . . . . *Dr.*	30,000	
	To 5% Debentures . . .		30,000
	Being call of balance due of £30 per debenture on 1,000 5% debentures issued at £95.		
Mar. 1	Debenture Discount . . . *Dr.*	5,000	
	To 5% Debentures		5,000
	Being discount of £5 per debenture on 1,000 5% debentures issued at £95.		

Dr.	FIVE PER CENT DEBENTURES		*Cr.*
			£
	Jan. 6	By Debentures Application and Allotment	65,000
	Mar. 1	,, Debentures Call .	30,000
		,, Debenture Discount .	5,000

Dr.	DEBENTURE APPLICATION AND ALLOTMENT						*Cr.*
			£				£
Jan. 6	To 5% Debentures .	J	65,000	Jan. 1	By Cash . .	CB	25,000
				6	,, do. . .	CB	40,000

Dr.   CALL ON DEBENTURES   **Cr.**

			£					£
Mar. 1	To 5% Debentures .		30,000	Mar. 1	By Cash .	.	CB	30,000

Dr.   DEBENTURE DISCOUNT   **Cr.**

			£					£
Mar. 1	To 5% Debentures .		5,000					

Dr.   CASH BOOK   **Cr.**

			£					£
Jan. 6	To Debenture Application and Allotment		65,000					
Mar. 1	,, Debentures Call . .		30,000					

Though the discount on debentures is a loss of loan capital, the liability of the company to the debenture-holders is the full nominal value of the debentures, and both the discount and the full nominal value of the debentures must appear in the Balance Sheet. The discount is shown temporarily as a *fictitious* asset until it is completely written off against profits.

BALANCE SHEET

	£		£
1,000 5% Debentures of £100 each . . .	100,000	Debenture Discount .	5,000

Debenture Stock

Debentures may be consolidated into one mass of debenture stock. Instead of 1,000 £100 debentures there could be £100,000 of debenture stock. Debenture stock must be fully paid, whereas debentures need not be fully paid up. The advantage is that debenture stock may be transferred in fractions, whereas debentures may be transferred only as a whole. £100 debentures of a company may be quoted at 80 on the Stock Exchange. An investor having £500 to invest may purchase six such debentures for £480 and will have £20 in hand. Had the security been debenture *stock* at 80 per £100 of stock, he would have been able to expend the whole £500 on £625 of debenture stock.

EXERCISE 58

On 1st May the London Stores Limited (registered with a share capital of 100,000 Ordinary shares of £1 each), offered 50,000 Ordinary shares of £1 each for public subscription, payable £0·15 per share on application, £0·85 per share on allotment. All the shares were applied for and allotted by 15th May and all moneys received.

Make the entries necessary to record the issue in the books of the company and show how the company's capital would appear in the Balance Sheet.

EXERCISE 59

The Wexford Company, Limited, has an authorized capital of £150,000 composed of 150,000 Ordinary shares of £1 each, of which 100,000 shares have already been issued, offers the remaining 50,000 shares for public subscription, payable—

25p. per share on application.
35p. „   „   on allotment.
40p. „   „   one month after allotment.

All the shares were subscribed and allotted and all cash received, including the call money.

Record these transactions in the books of the company and show how the capital would appear in the company's Balance Sheet.

EXERCISE 60

The Surrey Coal Company, Limited, was registered on 1st January with a nominal capital of 120,000 Ordinary shares of £1 each. On 1st February 100,000 shares were offered for public subscription, payable as follows—

On application, 20p. per share.
On allotment,   30p. „   „
On 15th March, 25p. „   „
On 15th May,   25p. „   „

All the shares offered were subscribed for and allotted and all money received on allotment and the first and final calls, except for the final call on 1,000 shares allotted to Edwin Brown.

Make the requisite entries in the company's books and show the capital as it would appear in the company's Balance Sheet.

EXERCISE 61

The Sussex Timber Company, Limited, was registered with an authorized capital of £150,000 made up of 50,000 6 per cent Preference shares of £1 each and 100,000 Ordinary shares of £1 each.

On 1st May subscriptions were invited for all these shares payable—

15p. per share on application.
35p. ,, ,, on allotment.
50p. ,, ,, on 1st July.

All the Preference and Ordinary shares were subscribed and allotted and all allotment and call money received.

Give the entries necessary in the books of the company and the capital as it would appear in the company's Balance Sheet.

EXERCISE 62

The Hampshire Stores, Limited, having a registered capital of £120,000 made up of 120,000 Ordinary shares of £1 each, decides to offer its unissued capital of 40,000 shares for public subscription to a premium of £0·25 per share, payable—

£0·15 per share on application.
£0·60 ,, ,, (including the premium) on allotment.
£0·50 ,, ,, one month after allotment.

All the shares were subscribed for and allotted and all the cash duly received. Make the entries necessary in the company's books and show the capital and the premium as it would appear in the company's Balance Sheet.

EXERCISE 63

The Directors of Dorsetshire, Limited, decided to offer the unissued part of its capital at a premium of £0·50 per share. The company's registered capital is 200,000 Ordinary shares of £1 each of which 150,000 have been issued and fully paid and 50,000 shares comprise the present issue. The offer was payable as follows—

£0·25 per share on application.
£0·75 ,, ,, on allotment (including the premium).
£0·50 ,, ,, one month after allotment.

All the shares were subscribed and duly allotted on 15th May. All the allotment instalments were paid by 17th May and the call money on 17th June.

Enter the details in the books of the company and show how the capital would appear in the company's Balance Sheet.

EXERCISE 64

Give the entries necessary to record in the books of Cornwall, Limited, the issue of 100 5 per cent debentures of £100 each, issued at 98. The whole amount due was payable on application.

Show the effect of this issue on the company's Balance Sheet.

EXERCISE 65

The Devon Mills, Limited, was registered with a nominal capital of £250,000, consisting of 50,000 6 per cent Preference shares of £1 each and 200,000 Ordinary shares of £1 each. All the capital was issued and fully paid. On 1st May, 19.., the Directors decide to offer for public subscription, 1,000 $5\frac{1}{2}$ per cent debentures of £100 each at a price of £105 per debenture, payable—

£20 on application.
£85, including the premium, on allotment.

The whole issue was subscribed and duly allotted and all cash received by 8th May.

Make the necessary entries in the company's books and show the capital and debentures as they would appear in the company's Balance Sheet.

EXERCISE 66

A company offered for public subscription £150,000 5 per cent debenture stock at 98, payable as follows—

On application,   £5 per £100 of stock.
On allotment,   £45 „   „   „   „
Two months later, £48 „   „   „   „

The issue was fully subscribed. The stock was allotted on 15th May, 19.., and all the money was received in due course.

Give the entries necessary to record the issue in the company's books, and show how the issue would stand in the company's Balance Sheet.

CHAPTER XV

COMPANY ACCOUNTS:
THE PROFIT AND LOSS ACCOUNT, APPROPRIATION
ACCOUNT, AND THE BALANCE SHEET

EVERY calendar year the directors must (under Sect. 148 of the Companies Act) lay before the company, that is the shareholders, in general meeting a Profit and Loss Account made up to a date within nine months prior to the date of meeting, and a Balance Sheet as at that date to which the Profit and Loss Account is made up. Attached to the Balance Sheet must be the Directors' Report on the last year's trading; their views on the prospects for the future; the amount they recommend as dividend, and the amounts proposed to be carried to reserve, etc.

Profit and Loss Account

For the most part the Profit and Loss Account of a company does not differ from that of a partnership or sole trading business; and students will do well to deal with it in two parts. In Part I will appear all the usual items such as Office Salaries, Carriage Outwards, and Rent on the debit side, and Discounts and Commissions Received on the credit side. At this point it can be ruled off and the balance brought down to Part II as *Net Trading Profit*.

In Part II of the Profit and Loss Account will appear items which affect the figure of profit for the year but which are not due to its routine trading, e.g. Directors' Remuneration, Auditors' Fees, Debentures and other Loan Interest, on the debit side; Income from Investments, amounts withdrawn from Provisions, etc., on the credit side. The balance will be *Net Profit (or Loss)* and will be carried down to the Appropriation Account.

The purpose of the Appropriation Account is to show what is done with the profit after it has been ascertained from the Profit and Loss Account. The undistributed profit from the last year is added (credited): the amounts placed to reserve and dividends paid or payable are deducted (debited). The balance of profit—and it is customary to leave as generous a margin as possible—is carried forward to next year.

Dividend

A dividend is a share of profit payable to the shareholders and is generally expressed as a percentage. Preference shares carry a fixed dividend, say 5 per cent or 6 per cent, but the directors declare the Ordinary share dividend according to the prosperity of the company. One year it may be 4 per cent, another year 12 per cent or 20 per cent.

Thus if a shareholder owned 1,000 £1 Ordinary shares in a company which was paying a dividend of 15 per cent he would be entitled to £150. The company would send him a *Dividend Warrant* (equivalent to a cheque) for this sum less Income Tax at the standard rate for that year.

In companies where the dividend remains fairly steady from year to year at something in the region of, for example, 12 per cent it is customary for the directors to declare an *Interim Dividend* of perhaps 6 per cent half-way through the financial year and a *Final Dividend* at the end of the year of, say, 7 per cent making a total dividend of 13 per cent for that year.

When the Interim Dividend is paid the bank will be credited with the amount due for all shareholders concerned and the Ordinary Dividend Account will be debited. At the end of the financial year the Ordinary Dividend Account will be credited and the Appropriation Account debited.

When the Final Dividend is declared at the end of the year the Appropriation Account is debited and the Ordinary Dividend Account is credited. As this dividend will not be paid until early next year the Ordinary Dividend Account has a credit balance which must appear on the Balance Sheet as a liability.

Dr.   ORDINARY SHARES DIVIDEND ACCOUNT   *Cr.*

			£				£
Jun. 30	To Bank	CB	12,500	Dec. 31	By Profit and Loss A/c (Appropriation Section) (Interim Dividend)	. L.F.	12,500
Dec. 31	,, Balance .	. c/d	25,000		,, Profit and Loss A/c (Appropriation Section) (Final Dividend)	. L.F.	25,000
			£37,500				£37,500
				Jan. 1	By Balance .	. b/d	25,000

(Income Tax Ignored)

The Balance Sheet

By Sect. 149 and the eighth schedule of the Act the Balance Sheet of a company must contain a summary of—

(*a*) The authorized share capital.

(*b*) The issued share capital.

(*c*) The liabilities and assets of the company which must be classified under headings appropriate to the company's business, distinguishing between the fixed assets and the current assets; and state

(*d*) How the value of the fixed assets has been arrived at.

Further, under separate headings, there must be stated, so far as they have not been written off—

(i) The preliminary expenses of the company.

(ii) Any expenses incurred in connexion with the issue of shares or debentures, or any amount paid by way of commission thereon.

(iii) The amount of goodwill, patents, or trade-marks if shown as a separate item in or ascertainable from the books of the company.

A company Balance Sheet should be set out to show the requisite information as follows—

BALANCE SHEET

AS AT ....

	£			£
Authorized Capital . . .		(i) *Fixed Assets*—		
Issued Capital . . .		Goodwill, Patents and		
Capital Reserves (Share Premium		Trade marks, Land and		
Account)		Buildings, etc. . .		
Revenue Reserves (Profit and Loss		(ii) *Investments*—		
Account balance) . .				
Long-term Liabilities (Debentures		(iii) *Current Assets*—		
and Loans) . . .		Payments in Advance		
Current Liabilities . .		(iv) *Fictitious Assets*— .		
Provisions . . .		Preliminary Expenses		
Dividends for Distribution .		Discount on Shares		
	£			£

EXERCISE 67

The trading profits of Mostyn's Limited, for the year ended 31st December, 19.., amounted to £32,100. The capital of the company is £200,000 consisting of 100,000 7 per cent Preference shares of £1 each, and 100,000 Ordinary shares of £1 each, both classes of shares being fully issued and paid up.

The Directors decide to allocate the profits as follows—

(a) To pay the Preference dividend for the year.
(b) To pay 15 per cent on the Ordinary shares.
(c) To write off the Preliminary Expenses (standing in the books at £3,000).
(d) To carry forward the balance.

Show the entries required on the assumption that this decision has been carried out. (Ignore Income Tax.)

EXERCISE 68

The Capital of Dobsons, Limited, is £100,000 divided into 50,000 6 per cent Preference shares of £1 each and 50,000 Ordinary shares of £1 each. All the capital is issued and fully paid.

The profits of the company for the year ended 31st December, 19.., amounted to £20,440, and £2,300 was brought forward from last year.

The Directors decide to make the following appropriations of profit—

1. To pay the Preference shares dividend for the year.
2. To pay a dividend of 20 per cent on the Ordinary shares.
3. To initiate a Reserve Account and to place £5,000 thereto.
4. To carry forward the balance to next year.

Give the entries (ignoring income tax) required to record this decision in the books of the company.

EXERCISE 69

You are required to prepare the Balance Sheet of a limited company as on the 31st December, 19.., from the following information: The Alma Manufacturing Company, Limited, was formed in the previous December, with a nominal capital of £80,000 in Ordinary shares of £1 each. Up to and including 31st December, 50,000 shares have been issued and fully paid with the exception of 160 shares on which 25p. per share was still unpaid.

Cash in hand, £100; Cash at bank, £3,400; Investments, £4,000; Sundry debtors, £16,281; Leasehold property, £6,700; Stock in hand, £36,297; Plant and machinery, £7,800; Goodwill, £10,000; Provision for bad and doubtful debts, £800; Sundry Creditors, £29,000; Interim dividend paid, £4,975; Profit for the year ending 31st December, 19.., £9,793.

(*N.C.T.E.C.*)

EXERCISE 70

The following is a list of the balances remaining in the books of Gamma Delta, Limited, after the Profit and Loss Account for the year to 30th April, 19.., has been written up and closed off—

	£
Preference shares, 30th April 19.. (authorized 50,000 of £1) 25,000 50p. paid	12,500
Call on above, 25p. per share	6,250
Calls unpaid on above	40
Ordinary shares, fully paid (authorized, 100,000 of £1)	80,000
Deferred shares, fully paid (authorized, 100,000 of £1)	8,000
Five per cent Debentures	36,000
Goodwill	10,000
Discount on Issue of Debentures	3,000
Sundry Debtors	40,939
Sundry Creditors—Trade	5,191
Freehold Premises	17,500
Sundry Creditors—Expenses	291
Rates paid in advance	316
Plant and Machinery Cost	72,000
Plant and Machinery—Provision for Depreciation	19,500
Fixtures and Fittings Cost	1,000
Fixtures and Fittings—Provision for Depreciation	365
Stock	19,873
Work in Progress	3,583
Bad Debts Provision	1,000
Profit and Loss Appropriation Account, 30th April *last* (Cr.)	2,492
Dividend on Preference shares to 30th April	375
Profit and Loss Account, year to *this* 30th April (Dr.)	5,946
Bank overdraft	3,124
Cash in hand	141

You are required to draw up the Balance Sheet of the company as on the closing date.

(*R.S.A.*)

EXERCISE 71

William Kay & Sons, Limited, was registered as a limited company in 19.., with a nominal capital of 25,000 Ordinary shares of £1 each; 22,000 of these had been issued and were fully paid with the exception of a call of £0·25 per share on 3,640 shares which is still unpaid. £3,000 6 per cent debentures had been issued at 97, repayable in ten years, and these were fully subscribed. In addition to the entries necessary to record the above the following balances were extracted from the books of the company on the 31st December, 19.. —

Dr.	£	Cr.	£
Leasehold Property	3,400	Reserve Account	4,500
Plant and Machinery	11,000	Sundry Creditors	29,600
Fixtures and Fittings	1,200	Repairs Reserve A/c	140
Stock in hand, 1st Jan.	11,100	Purchase Returns	1,800
Sundry Debtors	34,800	Sales	61,860
Cash at Bank	3,430	Profit and Loss A/c	9,200
Cash in hand	370	Discount	860
Purchases	43,800	Provision for Depreciation	
Salaries	3,500	on Plant and Machinery	2,500
Carriage on Sales	690	Provision for Depreciation	
Wages	6,820	of Fixtures and Fittings	500
Trade Expenses	1,400		
Rent, Rates and Taxes	3,000		
Insurance	400		
Gas and water	390		
Carriage on Purchases	690		
Sales Returns	3,400		
Bad Debts	90		
General Expenses	350		
Interest on debentures for			
the half-year to 30 June	90		
Discount	1,270		
Interim Dividend paid	2,100		
Travellers' commission	1,670		

You are required to prepare Trading and Profit and Loss Accounts for the year ended 31st December, 19.., and a Balance Sheet as on that date. Before preparing the final accounts the following information must be taken into consideration and the necessary adjustments journalized—

(a) The stock in hand on 31st Dec., 19.., was valued at £28,570.

(b) 10 per cent Depreciation is to be written off Plant and Machinery.

(c) Provide for half year's interest on debentures.

(d) $2\frac{1}{2}$ per cent to be provided on both Debtors and Creditors for discount thereon.

(e) £100 is to be added to Repairs Reserve Account.

(f) The Reserve Account is to be increased by £10,000.

(N.C.T.E.C.)

EXERCISE 72

The Paragon Manufacturing Company, Limited, was formed with a nominal capital of 100,000 Ordinary shares of £1 each; 75,000 of these had been issued and were fully paid, with the exception of a call of £0·25 on 2,000 shares which was still unpaid. £25,000 5 per cent Mortgage Debentures had also been issued at par, and were fully subscribed and paid. In addition to the entries necessary to record the above, the following balances were extracted from the books of the company on the 31st December, 19..—

Dr.	£	Cr.	£
Freehold Factory	45,600	Reserve Account	10,000
Bills Receivable	1,785	Sundry Creditors	10,185
Stock in hand, 1st Jan.	38,971	Sales	152,396
Machinery and Plant at cost	42,000	Purchase Returns	978
Investments	9,875	Bank overdraft	3,787
Debenture Interest	625	Bad Debts Provision	500
Directors' Fees	1,450	Interest on Investments	421
Office Furniture	750	Bills Payable	2,931
Profit and Loss Account—		Provision for Depreciation of	
Balance, 31st Dec.	1,327	Machinery	10,360
Sundry Debtors	10,740		
Purchases	106,943		
Factory Wages	15,876		
Office Salaries	3,241		
Office Expenses	768		
Rates & Taxes—Factory	1,028		
„ „ Office	295		
Power, Light and Heat—			
Factory	2,364		
Insurance—Factory	387		
„ Office	62		
Sales Returns	421		
Cash in hand	324		
Carriage Inwards	1,386		
Carriage Outwards	994		
Motor Lorries	3,846		

You are required to prepare Trading, and Profit and Loss Accounts for the year ending 31st December, 19.., and a Balance Sheet as on that date. Before preparing the final accounts the following information must be taken into consideration, and the necessary adjustments journalized—

(a) Depreciation is to be provided as follows: Machinery and Plant, 10 per cent; Office Furniture, 5 per cent.

(b) Expenses owing: Wages £184; Salaries, £38.

(c) The provision for doubtful debts is to be made to 5 per cent of the sundry debtors.

(d) The six months' interest on the debentures, due on the 31st December, 19.., has not been provided for.

(e) The following valuations were made on the 31st December, 19...
Stock in hand, £35,300; Motor Lorries, £3,452.

(N.C.T.E.C.)

EXERCISE 73

P., Ltd., is a manufacturing company having an authorized capital of
£160,000, divided into 50,000 7 per cent Preference shares, 100,000 Ordinary
shares, and 10,000 Deferred shares, all of £1 each.

The following was the Trial Balance extracted from the books as on 31st
January, 19...

TRIAL BALANCE

	£	£
30,000 Preference shares, fully paid		30,000
70,000 Ordinary shares, £0·75 called		52,500
Calls in Arrear (on Ordinary shares)	250	
10,000 Deferred shares, fully paid		10,000
General Reserve		10,000
Purchases, *less* Returns	39,207	
Bought Ledger Balances		3,595
Sales, *less* Returns		73,930
Sales Ledger Adjustment Account	11,449	
Wages and Salaries—Factory	15,372	
,, ,, Office	1,146	
Travellers' Salaries and Commission	3,530	
Rent (Factory $\frac{9}{10}$, Office $\frac{1}{10}$)	2,200	
Carriage Inwards	332	
Carriage Outwards	519	
Factory, Power and Expenses	2,370	
Rates, Heating, Lighting and Insurance—Factory	1,942	
,, ,, ,, —Office	227	
Machinery and Plant at Cost	68,200	
,, ,, Purchased during year	3,000	
Provision for Depreciation—1st Feb., 19...		10,000
Manufactured Stock, 31st Jan., 19..	21,518	
Raw materials, 31st Jan., 19..	5,163	
Postage, Stationery, and Office Expenses	510	
Office Fixtures and Fittings	620	
Legal Expenses and Audit Fee	325	
Directors' Fees	1,000	
Advertising	2,370	
Bank Interest		146
Discount		512
Dividends Unpaid		141
Interest on Calls in Arrear		25
Preliminary Expenses	2,100	
Carried forward	£183,350	£190,849

TRIAL BALANCE (contd.)

	£	£
Brought forward	183,350	190,849
Profit and Loss Account Balance 31st Jan., last .		11,242
Dividends Paid—		
On Preference shares, year to this 31st January.	2,100	
On Ordinary shares	5,250	
On Deferred shares	2,000	
Cash at Bank	9,146	
Cash in hand	245	
	£202,091	£202,091

You are required to prepare a Manufacturing Account and a Profit and Loss Account for the year ended 31st January, 19.., and a Balance Sheet as on that date, taking into consideration the following information and instructions—

(*a*) The Trial Balance of the Sales Ledger was as follows—

	£	£
Debit Balances	11,592	
Credit Balances		143
General Ledger Adjustment A/c . . .		11,449
	£11,592	£11,592

(*b*) Manufactured stock on hand on 31st January, 19.., was valued at £29,310, and raw materials were valued at £7,369.

(*c*) Depreciation on the old Plant and Machinery is to be written off at 8 per cent and on the new at 5 per cent, and the Office Fixtures and Fittings are to be depreciated 5 per cent.

(*d*) Unused Office Stationery, Stamps, etc., were valued on 31st January, 19.., at £19.

(*e*) £200 is to be reserved for rent due and unpaid, and £46 for travellers' commission.

(*f*) Half the balance of Preliminary Expenses is to be written off.

(*R.S.A.*)

CHAPTER XVI

COMPANY ACCOUNTS:
THE FORMATION OF A COMPANY TO ACQUIRE
AN EXISTING BUSINESS

IT frequently occurs that a limited liability company is formed for the express purpose of acquiring an existing business. The promoter of the company may be the present owner who wishes to take advantage of the principle of limited liability, or considers that the business is capable of extension if more capital is available. Sometimes the promoter of the company is interested only in its formation, and not in the particular business taken over. The offer to the public to subscribe for shares in the company brings in cash. The vendor, i.e. the seller, of the business may expect to be paid wholly in cash. Any balance of cash over and above the purchase price provides additional working capital. It is, however, more usual for the vendor to be paid partly in cash and partly in shares in the company. Sometimes the price is paid wholly in shares. It is apt to be interpreted as a lack of faith on the part of the vendor in the future of the business if he is to be paid wholly in cash. Being paid partly in shares the value of part of the purchase price depends upon the future success of the company.

The sale may include the business as a going concern. But whilst the assets are taken over, the liabilities may or may not be taken over according to the agreement. It may be left to the vendor to settle the liabilities. The cash, too, may or may not be taken over by the company according to the decision come to between the company and the vendor.

The purchase price may, of course, include payment for goodwill.

The book-keeping entries rendered necessary by the offer

and subscription of shares have been considered in Chapter XIV, and the purchase of a business in Chapter X. The student should refer to both chapters, as the only variation likely to occur from the procedure there discussed is the payment of the purchase price wholly or in part in shares instead of wholly in cash.

Example

Enterprise, Limited, was registered in 19.. with a nominal capital of £500,000, divided into 250,000 7 per cent Preference shares of £1 each and 500,000 Ordinary shares of £0·50 each.

The company was formed to acquire an established business, the purchase price £300,000, including Goodwill, being payable as follows: £50,000 in Preference shares, £50,000 in Ordinary shares (both fully paid), £100,000 in 4½ per cent Debenture Stock, and the balance in cash.

The balance of the Preference shares were subscribed by the public and fully paid up and 200,000 Ordinary shares were subscribed by the Directors and fully paid up.

The assets and liabilities taken over (at agreed values) were—

	£		£
Freehold Works . .	75,000	Plant and Machinery .	31,000
Stock	66,000	Sundry Debtors . .	112,000
Patents and Trade Marks . . .	8,000	Sundry Creditors . .	12,000

Give the Journal entries necessary to record the above transactions in the books of the company, and show its initial Balance Sheet.

(R.S.A.)

The excess of assets over liabilities taken over is £280,000. As the purchase price is £300,000, £20,000 of it represents payment for goodwill.

The purchase price is paid as to £200,000 by fully paid shares and debentures, and as to £100,000 by cash.

No cash is taken over, but £100,000 is received from subscriptions for the Ordinary shares, and £200,000 from subscriptions for the Preference shares. The total is £300,000, of which £100,000 is paid to the vendor, leaving £200,000 in hand.

The Preference shares are fully issued, but of the Ordinary shares 100,000 shares are allotted to the vendor as part purchase price, and 200,000 are taken up by the directors, leaving 200,000 shares of £0·50 each not issued.

JOURNAL

	£	£
Purchase of Business . . . *Dr.* To Vendor . . . . Being agreed purchase price of business .	300,000	300,000
Freehold Works . . . . *Dr.* Stock . . . . . Patents and Trade Marks . . Plant and Machinery . . Sundry Debtors . . . . Goodwill . . . . To Purchase of Business . . Being sundry assets acquired. .	75,000 66,000 8,000 31,000 112,000 20,000	312,000
Purchase of Business . . . *Dr.* To Sundry Creditors . . Being liabilities taken over. . .	12,000	12,000

Vendor . . . . . *Dr.*
  To Preference Share Capital
    (50,000 £1 shares) . .
  To Ordinary Share Capital
    (100,000 £0·50 shares) .
  To 4½% Debenture Stock
    (£100,000 Debenture Stock) .
Being Shares and Debenture Stock issued
  fully paid in part payment of purchase
  price. . . . . .
	200,000	50,000
		
		50,000
		
		100,000

Preference Shares Application and Allot-
  ment . . . . . *Dr.*
  To Preference Share Capital .
Being 200,000 £1 shares fully paid allotted
  by resolution of Directors dated . . . .
	200,000	200,000

Ordinary Share Application and Allot-
  ment . . . . . *Dr.*
  To Ordinary Share Capital .
Being 200,000 £0·50 shares fully paid allot-
  ted by resolution of Directors dated . . . .
	100,000	100,000

BALANCE SHEET OF ENTERPRISE, LTD.

	£	£		£	£
Authorized Capital—			*Fixed Assets—*		
250,000 7 % Preference			Goodwill . . .	20,000	
Shares of £1 each	250,000		Freehold Works	75,000	
500,000 Ordinary			Patents and Trade		
Shares of £0·50 each	250,000		Marks . .	8,000	
			Plant and Machinery .	31,000	
	£500,000				134,000
Issued Capital—			*Current Assets—*		
250,000 7 % Preference			Stock . . .	66,000	
Shares of £1 each	250,000		Sundry Debtors .	112,000	
300,000 Ordinary			Cash . .	200,000	
Shares of £0·50 each	150,000				378,000
		400,000			
Debentures—					
4½ % Debenture Stock		100,000			
Sundry Creditors		12,000			
		£512,000			£512,000

Not all the entries are shown unless the Cash Book is given or the cash transactions are journalized.

Dr.			CASH ACCOUNT		*Cr.*
		£			£
To Preference Shares			By Vendor (part purchase		
Application and			price) . . .		100,000
Allotment .		200,000	,, Balance . . . c/d		200,000
Ordinary Shares					
Application and					
Allotment .		100,000			
		£300,000			£300,000
To Balance . b/d		200,000			

EXERCISE 74

A limited company with a registered capital of £150,000 composed of 75,000 Ordinary shares of £1 each and 75,000 5½ per cent Preference shares of £1 each, was formed to acquire the existing business of Thomas Brown for £100,000, payable £50,000 in fully paid Ordinary shares, £25,000 in fully paid Preference shares and the remainder in cash.

The following assets and liabilities were taken over from Thomas Brown—

Assets	£
Cash	3,500
Debtors	27,500
Stock	15,000
Furniture and Fittings	3,000
Plant and Machinery	20,000
Freehold Premises	27,500
Current Liabilities	
Creditors	20,000

The balance of the Preference shares were offered to the public for subscription and were subscribed and fully paid up.

Show the Journal and Cash Book entries involved and the company's initial Balance Sheet.

EXERCISE 75

A limited company with an authorized capital of £75,000 in 75,000 Ordinary shares of £1 each was formed to acquire the existing business of Thomas Green, whose Balance Sheet at the agreed date of purchase was as below—

BALANCE SHEET

	£		£
Capital	30,000	Freehold Premises . .	15,000
Creditors . . .	3,500	Plant and Machinery .	8,000
Bills Payable . . .	1,500	Stock	5,000
		Debtors	3,000
		Bills Receivable . .	2,000
		Cash	2,000
	£35,000		£35,000

All the above assets and liabilities were taken over. The purchase price was £35,000, paid as to £25,000 in fully paid shares and as to £10,000 in cash.

25,000 shares were offered for public subscription and were duly subscribed and allotted and all money received.

Preliminary expenses paid amounted to £1,200.

Open the company's books and show the necessary entries and draft the initial Balance Sheet of the company.

EXERCISE 76

Woodcraft, Ltd., was registered to take over the business of Joseph Andrews at 31st December, 19. ., whose Balance Sheet at that date was as follows—

	£		£
Capital	14,917	Goodwill, Patents, etc. .	3,330
Creditors . . .	3,276	Plant	3,310
		Furniture, etc. . .	1,809
		Stock	5,491
		Debtors	4,108
		Cash at Bank . . .	145
	£18,193		£18,193

The purchase price was fixed at £13,500, payable as to £5,000 in cash, and £5,000 in fully paid Ordinary shares, and the balance in 7½ per cent debentures of £100 each.

The company took over all the assets and liabilities with the exception of the cash, debtors and creditors, and agreed to collect the debtors for the vendor and remit him the proceeds, less 2½ per cent collecting commission.

The shares and debentures were allotted on 1st January, 19.., on which date 20,000 Ordinary shares of £0·50 each were offered to the public, payable as to £0·25 per share on application and £0·25 per share on allotment.

Applications were received for 19,600 shares by 16th January, and these were duly allotted and the allotment moneys received by 30th January, on which date the balance of the purchase money was paid over to the vendor. On 31st January the vendor's debtors had all been collected and the amount due to the vendor was paid over. The formation expenses of the company, £642, were also paid on that date.

Open the books of Woodcraft, Ltd., and record the above transactions in Cash Book and Ledger Accounts, and prepare a Balance Sheet as at 31st January, 19...

Journal entries are not required, but all accounts should be presented.

(U.E.I.)

EXERCISE 77

The Chromium Steel Company, Ltd., having a nominal capital of £50,000 divided into 30,000 Ordinary shares of £1 each and 20,000 6 per cent Preference shares of £1 each, was formed to acquire the business of C. Barnby and Son as from 1st January, 19...

The purchase consideration was fixed at £20,000 for which tangible assets to the value of £15,000 were acquired.

On the following 31st December the purchase price had been discharged by the issue of £10,000 in fully paid Ordinary shares, £5,000 in 7 per cent debentures of £100 each, and the balance in cash. 7,500 Ordinary shares had been taken up by the public and fully subscribed with the exception of £62·50 calls in arrear, and 10,000 Preference shares had been issued and fully subscribed.

The following balances stood in the books of the company on 31st December, 19.., in addition to those indicated by the above transactions—

	£
Plant and Machinery	6,150·00
Salaries	1,938·00
Directors' Fees	1,000·00
Investments	3,010·00
Fixtures and Fittings	250·00
Carriage Inwards	397·00
Fuel, Light and Heating (Factory)	382·00
Freehold Factory	3,946·00
Wages	15,473·00
Manufacturing Expenses	964·50
Stock at 1st January	21,421·00
Rates and Insurance	968·00
Purchases	54,930·50

Sales	78,226·50
Returns Inwards	471·00
Returns Outwards	521·00
Discount Account (*Cr.*)	214·00
Bank Loan	2,412·00
Cash in hand	4,294·00
Creditors	20,353·00
Debtors	14,480·00
Office Expenses	647·00
Repairs to Buildings	686·00
Transfer Fees	6·00
Apprentices' Premiums (P. and L. Account)	250·00
Bad Debts	231·00
Provision for Bad and Doubtful Debts	400·00
Interest and Bank charges	98·00
Solicitors' Fees	125·00
Bills Payable	5,142·00
Motor Lorries	2,200·00
Loose Tools	900·00

Prepare Trading and Profit and Loss Accounts for the year ended 31st December, 19.., and a Balance Sheet at that date.

Make provision for the following—

1. Motor lorries were revalued at £1,760 and Loose Tools at £960.

2. Depreciation—Plant and Machinery 7½ per cent, Fixtures and Fittings 5 per cent.

3. Unexpired Rates and Insurance, £119.

4. Provision for Bad Debts to be made up to 5 per cent on the Debtors.

5. Debenture interest due (12 months).

6. Closing stock, £14,419.

(*U.E.I.*)

INDEX